climate change

HUMAN PERSPECTIVES AND GLOBAL IMPLICATIONS

Climate Change: Human Perspectives and Global Implications

© 2014 National Geographic Learning, Cengage Learning

Photographic Credit: cover
© Ralph Lee Hopkins/National Geographic Image Collection

For product information and technology assistance, contact us at
Cengage Learning Customer & Sales Support, 888-915-3276

For permission to use material from this text or product,
submit all requests online at **www.cengage.com/permissions.**
Further permissions questions can be emailed to
permissionrequest@cengage.com.

ISBN: 978-12851-94462

National Geographic Learning
1880 Oak Avenue, Suite 300
Evanston, IL 60201
USA

Cengage Learning products are represented in Canada by
Nelson Education, Ltd.

Visit National Geographic Learning online at **NGL.cengage.com**
Visit our corporate website at **www.cengage.com.**

Printed in the USA.
RR Donnelley, Jefferson City, MO

12 13 14 15 16 17 18 19 20 21 22

10 9 8 7 6 5 4 3 2 1

Table *of* Contents

About the Series

Cengage Learning and National Geographic Learning are proud to present the *National Geographic Learning Reader Series*. This groundbreaking series is brought to you through an exclusive partnership with the National Geographic Society, an organization that represents a tradition of amazing stories, exceptional research, first-hand accounts of exploration, rich content, and authentic materials.

The series brings learning to life by featuring compelling images, media, and text from National Geographic. Through this engaging content, students develop a clearer understanding of the world around them. Published in a variety of subject areas, the *National Geographic Learning Reader Series* connects key topics in each discipline to authentic examples and can be used in conjunction with most standard texts or online materials available for your courses.

How the reader works

Each article is focused on one topic relevant to the discipline. The introduction provides context to orient students and focus questions that suggest ideas to think about while reading the selection. Rich photography, compelling images, and pertinent maps are amply used to further enhance understanding of the selections. The chapter culminating section includes discussion questions to stimulate both in-class discussion and out-of-class work.

An eBook will accompany each reader and will provide access to the text online with a media library that may include images, videos, and other content specific to each individual discipline.

Few organizations present this world, its people, places, and precious resources in a more compelling way than National Geographic. Through this reader series we honor the mission and tradition of National Geographic Society: to inspire people to care about the planet.

Despite being a hotly debated and highly contentious subject, global climate change has emerged as one of the most significant threats and challenges of our time. Although we are dependent on greenhouse gases such as carbon dioxide to keep the planet warm and amenable to life, the hyper-accumulation of such gases that results from the burning of fossil fuels and the clearing of forests can have a disruptive effect on the climate. In the absence of human activities, greenhouse gases are responsible for trapping a certain amount of solar radiation and keeping the planet from freezing. As gases are added to the atmosphere, the insulating properties are exacerbated and warming ensues.

Although it may seem that the study of climate change is somewhat new, the issue has been the object of scientific inquiry for many decades. As the first article in this collection indicates, serious scientific concern over anthropogenic climate change was already being addressed over 20 years ago. Regularly collected data goes back much further than that, and scientists have been able to reliably reconstruct the earth's climate going back many thousands of years. This article will give a historical perspective to the issue and give an indication of what the state of the science was before climate change was well-known to the general public. It also addresses the challenges facing the effort to use modeling to meaningfully predict the effects of greenhouse gas accumulation in the atmosphere on the future of the climate.

The remaining articles in the reader all take the reality of anthropogenic influences on global climate as a point of departure. In acknowledging that human activities are a major driver of climate change, it is necessary to evaluate the activities that cause that impact and appraise the alternatives that would lead to its alleviation. The second article in this selection does just that, in a very readable first-person exploration of the use of household energy and the means by which individuals may minimize their contribution to global climate change. As such, the article invites the reader to take responsibility for the issue, and begs the question that leads so many to take no action at all: do the activities of one person really matter?

The impacts of global climate change are many and varied. They include increased severity of storms, droughts and wildfires as well as the oft-cited predicted rise in sea level that could potentially inundate many coastal regions around the globe. The main storehouses of that ice that is predicted to melt and lead to sea level rise are Antarctica and Greenland. The third piece in this series of articles surveys the many perspectives of the people of Greenland who will be impacted. As a nation that has very limited access to resources given the expansive ice sheet covering much of the landmass, their future may be considerably bright, even as the rest of the world confronts the rising sea. This article looks deeply into the social implications of a people who are on the front-lines of the climate change crisis.

As Greenland melts, the low-lying nations of the world will feel the effects to the greatest extent, particularly those that are also mired in poverty. The fourth article covers the impacts of climate change on Bangladesh as the people of that country confront the reality of rising seas and intensifying storms with a resilience born of a long history of strife; a resilience that the article suggests may be just what the world needs to confront the coming impacts of a changing climate.

This series of articles concludes with a look at the opportunities the world has to develop solutions to the climate change crises. As the world's most rapidly developing economy, China has made great strides toward sustainability. Nevertheless, it now produces greater carbon emissions than any other country largely due to a heavy reliance on coal. This final piece explores the opposing forces of fossil fuels and sustainable energy. It also highlights the tremendous opportunities the developing world has to integrate sustainable technologies into their growing infrastructure. China's magnificent economic growth remains a wild card in the future of the global climate change issue.

As a whole, these articles cover many facets of the incredibly diverse causes and impacts of climate change. They represent many perspectives, from atmospheric science to the societies most affected, and from the deep past to the not so distant future. Collectively, they provide a meaningful look at one of the world's most pressing scientific and social issues.

UNDER THE SUN

Over two decades ago, it was readily acknowledged that the earth's climate was changing and that the massive accumulation of greenhouse gases in the atmosphere was influencing this process. Although it may seem that the climate change discussion has its beginnings quite recently, the topic actually has deep roots. National Geographic originally covered the topic in the 1970's and the following article, from 1990, offers a comprehensive summary of the state of the science and debate. As you read the article, pay particular attention to the level of agreement amongst scientists and the points on which there is dissent.

As you read "Under the Sun," consider the following questions:

- What pattern has the carbon dioxide level in the atmosphere shown over time?
- What role does carbon dioxide play in keeping the planet warm?
- What were the limitations to using computer models to predict future effects of climate change circa 1990?
- What are the effects of cloud cover, the capacity of the oceans to absorb carbon and variation in solar energy over time on the ability of climatologists to accurately predict the effects of climate change?
- To what extent is climate change thought to arise from anthropogenic causes—that is, causes derived from the activities of human societies?

The sun sets behind Colorado's front range. Five-inch telescope image by Joseph Sutorik, Space Environment Services Center/NOAA, Boulder, Colorado.

UNDER
THE
SUN

By Samuel W. Matthews

Photographs by James A. Sugar

Their faces to the setting sun, mirror-winged solar panels convert even the last rays of the day directly into electricity. These southern California collectors add a clean and inexhaustible energy source to the state's power grid.

FOR MORE THAN FOUR BILLION YEARS THE SUN AND THE EARTH ITSELF HAVE BEEN THE DRIVING FORCES IN OUR PLANET'S CHANGING CLIMATE.

NOW WE PUNY HUMANS—IN ALL OUR BILLIONS—

MAY HAVE BECOME THE DECISIVE FORCE FOR CHANGE IN THE DECADES AHEAD.

As Pogo put it, the enemy is us.

The road up earth's most massive mountain—Mauna Loa on the Big Island of Hawaii—is a narrow, twisting strip of tar, laid by prison labor through raw, jagged lava fields. You can drive it—with great caution and constant awe—to a small cluster of white and blue huts standing more than two miles high in the clear, cool Pacific sky.

Here for 32 years the level of carbon dioxide in the earth's atmosphere has been recorded daily at the Mauna Loa Observatory by Charles David Keeling of the Scripps Institution of Oceanography and by scientists from the National Oceanic and Atmospheric Administration (NOAA). And for 32 years the level has risen, in a wavy curve of spring-fall variations (opposite), from 315 parts per million (ppm) in 1958 to more than 355 in mid-1990.

That steadily climbing CO_2 level (air locked in glacial ice a century ago held only about 280 ppm—25 percent less) is an incontrovertible measure of what man and his machines have done to the atmosphere of the earth in scarcely one lifetime. Because of it, say many scientists who study the climate, our planet is bound to become warmer—has already warmed—as more and more energy from the sun is caught and held in the thin blanket of air around us.

"As Pogo put it, the enemy is us," said Elmer Robinson, director of Mauna Loa Observatory, while we drove together up the desolate slope of the volcano. "By burning more and more fossil fuel—gasoline, natural gas, coal, peat—even ordinary firewood, we are putting into the air more of the gases that act much like a globe of glass around the planet. That's what's called the greenhouse effect.

"Up here we measure not only CO_2," he went on, as he led me through a laboratory jammed with humming recorders and glowing computer terminals. "We also read methane, chloro-fluorocarbons, nitrous oxide, and ozone, all of which add to the warming. We see and measure dust of various sizes in the troposphere, the weather layer of the atmosphere."

Such data, recorded by NOAA here and at American Samoa in mid-Pacific, at Point Barrow in Alaska, and at the South Pole, form the hard evidence on which (Continued on page 10)

Adapted from "Under the Sun: Is Our World Warming?" by Samuel W. Matthews: National Geographic Magazine, October 1990.

The power of sunlight captured millions of years ago by plants and animals and buried in huge deposits is now being burned as coal, petroleum, and natural gas. Such burning in power stations, automobiles, and homes releases carbon dioxide (CO_2) to the air. Once airborne, CO_2 absorbs heat, warming the atmosphere in the so-called greenhouse effect.

RUSH HOUR ON THE BAY BRIDGE IN OAKLAND

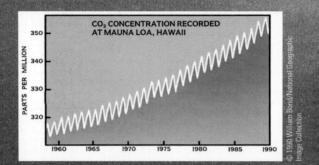

An unusual sight in San Francisco, smog hides the city only four or five days a year. Far more ominous: the invisible but relentless rise of carbon dioxide in the atmosphere. Scientists on Hawaii's Mauna Loa, two miles above the Pacific Ocean, have recorded a steady increase in the global concentration of CO_2 since 1958 (graph above). The zigzag pattern reflects the seasonal growth and dieback of plants, which soak up prodigious amounts of CO_2 during spring and summer.

A century ago CO_2 measured 280 parts per million, according to analysis of air trapped in ice sheets. Scientists say this evidence shows the effects of human activities such as burning fossil fuels. Most believe the rising CO_2 level will lead to higher global temperatures and significant climate change.

(*Continued from page 5*) climatologists base widely varying and controversial visions of the future. Average temperature worldwide, by careful calculations, has gone up about half a degree Celsius—one degree Fahrenheit—since the late 1800s.

In this century, the decade of the 1980s saw the six warmest years in weather records. Yet there are some researchers and statisticians who argue this apparent warming of the planet may be only a temporary blip, that natural warming periods have occurred before, without man's intervention, and that there is as yet no sure evidence of long-term change.

All this was in my mind under the blaze of sunlight that beautiful winter day atop Mauna Loa. Through a small occulting telescope maintained there by the National Center for Atmospheric Research at Boulder, Colorado, I stared at the darkened face of the sun, ringed by its glowing, gauzy corona.

From that blazing disk high in the Hawaiian sky comes the endless power that drives and rules all life on earth: its plant growth and the food chains of all its creatures; the winds, rains, and churning weather of the planet; the ocean currents, forests, prairies, and deserts.

Our home star in the heavens burns steadily, almost without variation. It is the "almost," coupled with what man's activities are doing to the atmosphere, that this story is about. It is becoming more and more apparent that the effects of the sun upon our planet are changing. Our one and only home may be in harm's way, and we can scarcely sense just what is happening—or know what to do about it.

That burning energy of our sun works the miracle on earth called photosynthesis. Powered by sunlight, plants green with chlorophyll combine carbon dioxide from the air with water from soil or sea into energy-rich carbohydrates, releasing into the atmosphere the oxygen we need to breathe.

It is the same process by which primitive bacteria of ocean shallows, more than two billion years ago, first produced enough oxygen to permit other life on earth to develop. And it is the same process—still imperfectly understood—that grows the corn of Iowa, the grass of your lawn, the rain forests of Brazil, the floating plankton that sustains life in the seas.

French mathematician Jean Fourier in 1822 compared the earth's atmosphere to the glass of a greenhouse: Both let the sun's visible rays enter to warm land, water, plants, and air, yet retard the escape of heat. His comparison was apt—in part. Without its atmosphere, the earth would be as frozen and lifeless as Mars, instead of averaging 15°C (59°F) and sustaining millions of species. Although the physics of earth's atmosphere and greenhouse glass are quite different, the term caught on even before British engineer G.S. Callendar warned in 1938 that human activities were altering this beneficial greenhouse effect.

What causes this warming, when 99 percent of the atmosphere is nitrogen and oxygen, neither of which absorbs much heat? Scientists have discovered that water vapor, carbon dioxide, and other gases—though mere traces in the air—act as powerful heat absorbers. Today the greenhouse effect stands as well established as any theory in the atmospheric sciences, anchored by countless measurements from satellites, weather balloons, and ground stations.

"Without carbon dioxide in the atmosphere, life as we know it would be impossible," Elmer Robinson had said on Mauna Loa. "We couldn't exist if it weren't for greenhouse warming."

About half of the radiant energy reaching earth from the sun, because of its short wavelengths, can pass through the atmosphere to the earth's surface. But the longer waves of heat that radiate back toward space are absorbed and reradiated by water vapor, carbon dioxide, other gases, and clouds, and the atmosphere warms.

"That's the greenhouse effect," Elmer had said. "Without it, earth would be frozen—at least 60 degrees Fahrenheit colder—and there would be no more life here than on Mars. But if it were to increase.... Well, some climatologists say we face temperatures three to nine degrees higher in the next century."

Back in the last glacial age, some 20,000 years ago, world temperature averaged about nine degrees colder than today. The carbon dioxide level was only 190 to 200 parts per million, ancient ice samples from Greenland and Antarctica show. As the ice melted back, the CO_2 level gradually rose to about 280 ppm by the beginning of the industrial age.

"By the middle of the coming century—in our children's lifetime," Elmer had said, "the level will reach 550 or even 600 at its current rate of rise."

The prospect of doubled CO_2—and even more rapid rise of other gases, such as methane, which together equal the warming effect of CO_2 in the atmosphere—is what has atmospheric scientists urgently refining their computer models of the climate.

World population also is predicted to double by the middle of the next century, from five billion people to ten. And as all nations become more developed and use more fuel to support those people, the release of carbon dioxide and other gases to the air is bound to keep increasing—despite the care taken or which fuels are burned.

With more warmth and more CO_2, some ask, would not more crops grow, in wider areas than today? Would we not benefit from a warmer world?

Without carbon dioxide in the atmosphere, life as we know it would be impossible.

Perhaps, in some areas. The more CO_2 in the air, the more productive some plants become. But the biggest unknown is what changes would occur in the planet's weather patterns.

Most climate models show that in some regions—northern Scandinavia, Siberia, and Canada, for example—more rain would fall and more trees and crops grow. But in today's great mid-continent breadbasket regions, warming would lead to the drying of soil in summer. Destructive droughts, such as that of 1988 in North America, would strike more often, until the Great Plains and Ukraine turn semidesert. Storms such as hurricanes and tornadoes might become more violent. Forests would decline and change under the temperature rise, and wildlife would have to migrate—if it could—or perish. The permafrost under Arctic tundra would thaw, deep peatlands would decompose, and vast new amounts of carbon dioxide and methane could be released.

And just as inevitably, as ocean waters warm and expand and the ice on Greenland and Antarctica melts back, the seas would creep higher onto the edges of the continents. Large parts of such low countries as Bangladesh—already swept by ruinous floods and typhoons—would be submerged; cities like Miami, Venice, even New York, would cower behind dikes.

"If a rise of one to three feet, as the models have predicted, seems extreme," says environmental scientist Stephen Leather-man of the University of Maryland, "keep in mind that the oceans rose more than 300 feet after the last ice age—all in only a few thousand years."

If the ice cap on the island of Greenland were to melt completely, glaciologists estimate the oceans would rise another 20 feet. Sea level in the eastern *(Continued on page 15)*

Earth's thermostat: the greenhouse effect

1 NATURAL GREENHOUSE

As radiation from the sun (yellow) enters earth's atmosphere, a portion of it is reflected back into space or absorbed directly by the atmosphere. The 50 percent or so that reaches the ground is converted into infrared radiation, or heat (red). Clouds and greenhouse gases such as water vapor and CO_2 absorb most of the heat that the earth radiates back toward space. These gases then reradiate the heat. Over time, the outgoing radiation balances the incoming.

Other energy (orange) includes latent heat released by formation of clouds and convective heat carried by updrafts.

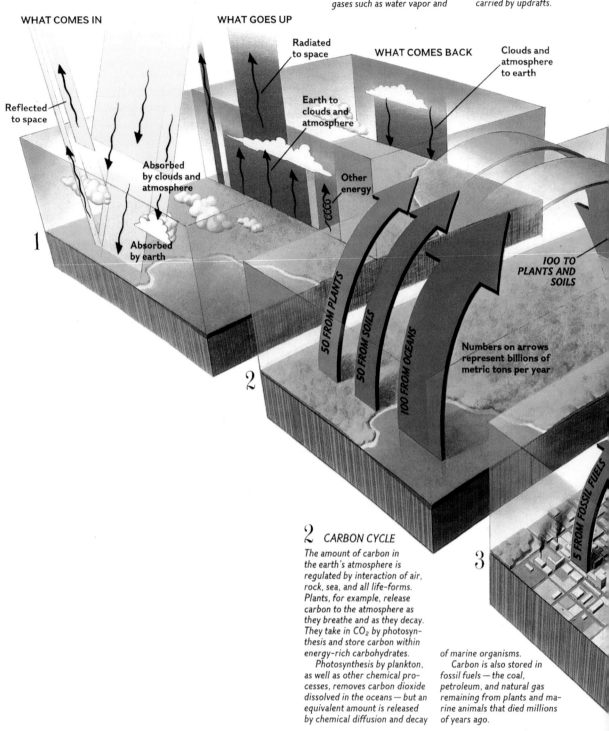

WHAT COMES IN

WHAT GOES UP

WHAT COMES BACK

Reflected to space

Radiated to space

Earth to clouds and atmosphere

Clouds and atmosphere to earth

Absorbed by clouds and atmosphere

Other energy

Absorbed by earth

1

2

50 FROM PLANTS

50 FROM SOILS

100 FROM OCEANS

100 TO PLANTS AND SOILS

Numbers on arrows represent billions of metric tons per year

3

5 FROM FOSSIL FUELS

2 CARBON CYCLE

The amount of carbon in the earth's atmosphere is regulated by interaction of air, rock, sea, and all life-forms. Plants, for example, release carbon to the atmosphere as they breathe and as they decay. They take in CO_2 by photosynthesis and store carbon within energy-rich carbohydrates.

Photosynthesis by plankton, as well as other chemical processes, removes carbon dioxide dissolved in the oceans — but an equivalent amount is released by chemical diffusion and decay of marine organisms.

Carbon is also stored in fossil fuels — the coal, petroleum, and natural gas remaining from plants and marine animals that died millions of years ago.

PAINTING BY MARK SEIDLER; CONSULTANTS: ROBERT C. HARRISS, UNIVERSITY OF NEW HAMPSHIRE; ALAN ROBOCK, UNIVERSITY OF MARYLAND

ART AND DIAGRAMS FOR THIS ARTICLE
DESIGN: ALLEN CARROLL; RESEARCH: WENDY CORTESI, LISA R. RITTER, DAVID W. WOODDELL

3 HUMAN INFLUENCES

Humans have disrupted the natural carbon cycle by burning fossil fuels for energy and by clearing forests to feed and house growing populations. Yearly about 50 million acres of forest are lost to logging, farming, and pasturage.

Industrial and agricultural emissions raise atmospheric carbon by about seven billion metric tons a year. Roughly half is absorbed by the oceans and by vegetation and soils.

Emission of greenhouse gases can be reduced, but no technology is available to remove them once they reach the atmosphere.

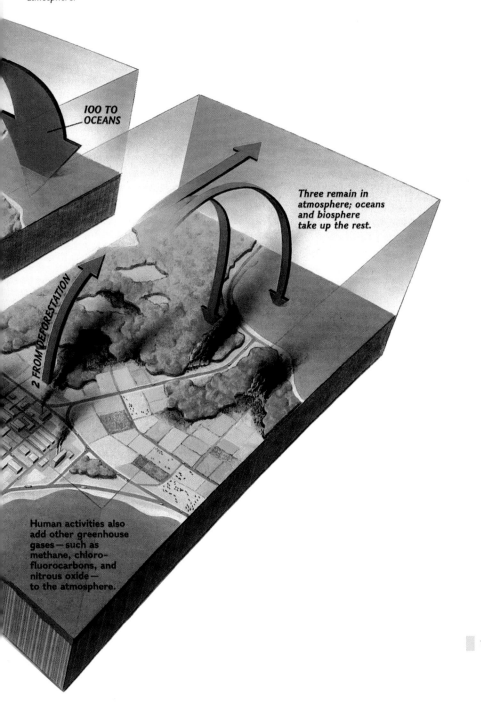

100 TO OCEANS

2 FROM DEFORESTATION

Three remain in atmosphere; oceans and biosphere take up the rest.

Human activities also add other greenhouse gases — such as methane, chloro-fluorocarbons, and nitrous oxide — to the atmosphere.

On the road to understanding sources of methane, scientists from the National Center for Atmospheric Research in Boulder, Colorado, test what turned out to be an innocent suspect fresh asphalt. Wide ranging research suggests that leaks and venting from coal, oil, and natural gas production may be underestimated.

Cattle, a known source of methane, are increasing world wide—faster than the human population. The same bacteria that enable a cow to turn grass into meat or milk cause it to expel methane, roughly 14 cubic feet a day.

(Continued from page 11) United States has already risen a foot in this century alone, and it is predicted to go up at least another foot in the century ahead. With that one-foot rise, Leatherman says, the high-water line at Ocean City, Maryland, will move inland 100 to 200 feet; in Florida, 200 to 1,000 feet; in Louisiana, several miles.

Yet paradoxically, say other glaciologists, the huge ice domes on both Greenland and Antarctica may not be shrinking but growing. The paradox is that this too may be a sign of global warming. As the atmosphere warms, it holds more water vapor from evaporation of oceans and soil; hence more snow falls in the polar regions, hence more ice and possibly lower sea levels. But the warmer seas eventually will melt back the fringes of the polar ice, and the oceans will creep inexorably higher.

Foretelling what may happen to the world if it should warm by even one or two degrees is the toughest problem facing climatologists today. Even though there have been times in the dim geologic past when temperatures were warmer—with no ice at all on the polar regions—there are vast differences today. No one knows whether the "wild card" of human activity will disrupt or make more extreme the cycles ordained by nature.

To try to predict the effects of human intervention, scientists mathematically simulate the weather systems of the globe. Their equations, called general circulation models (GCMs), are so complex that only a few of today's supercomputers can solve them.

The equations relate such things as the balance of radiation to and from the planet, air circulation, evaporation and rainfall, ice cover, sea-surface temperature—then try to assess what might happen if the sun were to become brighter by a tiny amount or if the carbon dioxide in the atmosphere gradually doubles as expected. The computers then calculate and map the changes in the weather of future days, weeks, seasons—or centuries.

One key to their accuracy lies in how finely they divide the planet's surface, the blanket of the atmosphere, and the seas. Most now divide the globe into blocks of at least five degrees of latitude and five of longitude: 300 nautical miles on a side, roughly the size and shape of Colorado. The best models then divide the atmosphere into as many as 20 layers and add in the oceans' currents and multiple layers. The computations are so formidable that a supercomputer might take a week to run a single change of input to determine its effect.

On a high shelf of Colorado's front range, where deer roam in the open above the university town of Boulder, stand the sand-hued buildings of the National Center for Atmospheric Research (NCAR), one of the principal climate-modeling centers in the nation. The others are NASA's Goddard Institute for Space Studies (GISS) on upper Broadway in New York City and NOAA's Geophysical Fluid Dynamics Laboratory (GFDL) in Princeton, New Jersey.

The computer room at NCAR, its floor carpeted with bright red squares, is a futuristic assemblage of multicolored cabinets, computer terminals, and blinking panels of lights. The chief of the center, Bill Buzbee, showed me two red-and-black cylinders, each about five feet in diameter and five feet high, with segments seemingly cut out of them like huge wedges of cheese.

"Those are our Cray supercomputers," Bill said. "Not many exist in the world. If you'd like to buy one, it might cost you about 20 million bucks. And it would not be powerful enough for much of the modeling we're asked to do."

"If our global grid were reduced to two and a half degrees on a side and the number of vertical layers increased," I had heard Jerry

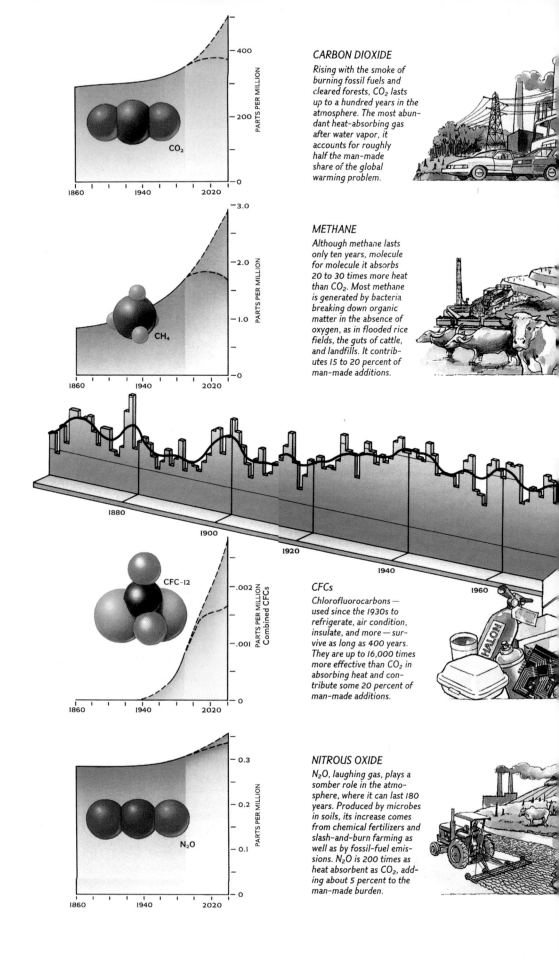

CARBON DIOXIDE

Rising with the smoke of burning fossil fuels and cleared forests, CO_2 lasts up to a hundred years in the atmosphere. The most abundant heat-absorbing gas after water vapor, it accounts for roughly half the man-made share of the global warming problem.

CO_2

METHANE

Although methane lasts only ten years, molecule for molecule it absorbs 20 to 30 times more heat than CO_2. Most methane is generated by bacteria breaking down organic matter in the absence of oxygen, as in flooded rice fields, the guts of cattle, and landfills. It contributes 15 to 20 percent of man-made additions.

CH_4

CFCs

Chlorofluorocarbons — used since the 1930s to refrigerate, air condition, insulate, and more — survive as long as 400 years. They are up to 16,000 times more effective than CO_2 in absorbing heat and contribute some 20 percent of man-made additions.

CFC-12

NITROUS OXIDE

N_2O, laughing gas, plays a somber role in the atmosphere, where it can last 180 years. Produced by microbes in soils, its increase comes from chemical fertilizers and slash-and-burn farming as well as by fossil-fuel emissions. N_2O is 200 times as heat absorbent as CO_2, adding about 5 percent to the man-made burden.

N_2O

Fever chart of a warming planet

Global temperature is like a mortgage rate: Over time a slight change can make a big difference. After about A.D. 1350 a drop of 0.5°C (1°F) starved out Norse settlements in Greenland and forced farmers in Europe to abandon fields. Since the mid-1800s, with increasing industrialization, average global temperature has risen by 0.5°C.

Some scientists link that recent rise directly to the heat-absorbing gases that humans have released to the atmosphere. Other scientists are less certain,

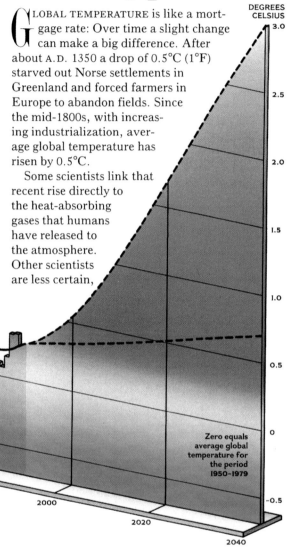

DEGREES
CELSIUS

3.0

2.5

2.0

1.5

1.0

0.5

0

Zero equals
average global
temperature for
the period
1950-1979

-0.5

2000

2020

2040

stressing natural variability and changes in solar output. Few, however, doubt that the changing composition of the atmosphere will lead to some warming.

The graphs (left) project future accumulations of greenhouse gases along two lines—with business as usual and with aggressive actions to limit release. Projected temperature increases (above) range from 0.7°C to 3°C by 2040.

HISTORICAL TEMPERATURE GRAPH: UNIVERSITY OF EAST ANGLIA, U.K.

PAINTINGS BY NGS STAFF ARTISTS WILLIAM H. BOND AND CHRISTOPHER A.
KLEIN (MOLECULES); GRAPHS BY DALE GLASGOW
ART CONSULTANTS: BARBARA BRAATZ, ICF INC.; ALAN ROBOCK
GAS GRAPH DATA: R. A. HOUGHTON AND G. M. WOODWELL, WOODS HOLE
RESEARCH CENTER; ICF INC., FOR EPA; NASA/GISS; G. I. PEARMAN,
COMMONWEALTH SCIENTIFIC AND INDUSTRIAL RESEARCH CORPORATION

Mahlman, director of GFDL, say, "it would multiply the demand on the computer 16-fold; at one degree square, which might be necessary to forecast weather and climate accurately for local regions on the globe, the order of complexity—and computer time—would go up at least 500 times."

I began to appreciate what these machines do. They reduce inconceivably complicated systems of the atmosphere and oceans to logical, mathematical predictions of what might happen if man or nature changes the ways things are with the world.

All the most advanced GCMs, fed a doubling of carbon dioxide, come up with similar results: The world will warm by the middle of the next century by two to five degrees Celsius—three to nine degrees Fahrenheit—with even greater warming in the subpolar latitudes. The differences between the models show up in regional effects: exactly where drying or more rainfall may occur, whether the Northern and Southern Hemispheres may react differently.

The modelers acknowledge they may be as much as a decade away from full confidence in their results. At GFDL they have been trying for 20 years to couple ocean circulation to the atmosphere. Syukuro Manabe, one of GFDL's most noted modelers, admits that in the early days "all sorts of crazy things happened [in the computer]. . . sea ice covered the tropical oceans, for example."

Another noted climate modeler—and spokesman for potential trouble—is James Hansen, director of NASA's Goddard Institute (GISS) in New York City. During the scorching hot, dry summer of 1988 he captured international attention when he testified before a Senate subcommittee.

"The world is getting warmer," he said bluntly. "We can state with 99 percent confidence that current temperatures represent a real global warming trend, rather than a chance fluctuation. We will surely have more years like this—more droughts and many more days above a hundred degrees—in the 1990s.ʺ

He repeated these predictions in subsequent scientific meetings and climate symposiums—upsetting colleagues who felt he should hedge his concerns with more qualifications and maybes. But that is not Jim Hansen's way.

Some have heard and heeded what he and others have been saying. Senator Albert Gore, Jr., of Tennessee, one of the most outspoken politicians calling for action in the face of world warming, has said bluntly: "The greenhouse effect is the most important environmental problem we have ever faced. [It threatens] loss of forests, widespread drought and famine, loss of wild species . . . topsoil, stratospheric ozone. . . . Do we have the capacity, the will, to change habits of millennia in a generation?"

Stephen H. Schneider of NCAR, an intense, curly-haired prophet of the future, has been deeply involved in climate research for more than 20 years. He writes, speaks, and travels incessantly; he is one of the worried scientists to whom policymakers listen carefully.

"I agree with Jim Hansen and others that the world has gotten warmer over the past century—faster than ever since about 1975," he told me. "I'm not so quick to say it's entirely due to the greenhouse effect—though that's certainly there. Natural climate variations may be at work too, reinforcing—or at other times masking—the greenhouse forcing. In coming decades some years and some parts of the world may be cooler, but others will be much warmer than normal.

"The 1988 drought in North America, for example, has been linked by colleagues at NCAR with the El Niño phenomenon of the tropical Pacific Ocean. A shift in the jet stream, caused by massive ocean-atmosphere interactions in the Pacific, was the likely cause of

The world is getting warmer. We can state with 99 percent confidence that current temperatures represent a real global warming trend, rather than a chance fluctuation.

that hot, extremely dry summer.

"But whatever the local and temporary weather changes, the world can't wait for proof of warming before trying to do something about it. We're engaged in a huge experiment, using our earth as the laboratory, and the experiment is irreversible. By the time we find the greenhouse warming has damaged earth's ability to feed its people, it will be too late to do much about it."

What would he have us do about it now? Try to slow the release of greenhouse gases—by more rigorous energy conservation and changes in fuel use (natural gas releases half as much CO_2 as coal); by reducing the burning of rain forests, which increases the level of CO_2 in the air; and by planting many more trees, wherever possible.

"Keep in mind, it's not only carbon dioxide that's at fault," Steve Schneider points out. "Methane, which is released from decomposing tundra and marshes, rice fields, termites, and the guts of cattle, is increasing in the atmosphere faster than CO_2, at something like one percent a year. And molecule for molecule it has 20 to 30 times the greenhouse effect of CO_2. Nitrogen gases, from fertilizers as well as car exhausts and factory smokestacks, chlorofluorocarbons (CFCs) and other industrial products—all the other gases we're pouring into the air—are already doubling the warming potential of CO_2 alone.

"We can hope to reduce some of them, such as the CFCs that attack stratospheric ozone," he said. "But the others go with the industrial development of the world; all we can realistically hope is to slow their release, to gain time to cope with the results.

"If we can delay a 2°C increase of global temperature from 2025 to 2050, we will have more time to develop alternate energy sources: Nuclear—possibly fusion—is one option, despite its problems. But tapping the sun directly, by solar heat plants and converting sunlight directly into electricity, is both possible and coming down in cost."

I was to see his future in California, at the Rancho Seco nuclear plant outside Sacramento, flanked by 20 acres of solar panels slowly swinging with the sun across the sky; at a pioneering solar-cell factory near Los Angeles, where a breakthrough in "thin-film" technology was closing in on conventional electric power costs; and on a treeless mountain pass above Oakland, where a seemingly endless array of propellers taps the sun's energy from the winds sweeping in off the Pacific.

Computer forecasting of climate is uncertain for reasons other than the sheer complexity of the equations. There are variables and feedbacks that even the best of the models barely approach.

The oceans are the chief reservoir of heat, controlling weather over the entire globe. As currents such as the Gulf Stream carry the heat from the tropics to high latitudes, cold water from the polar regions sinks and flows toward the Equator, overturning the seas about every thousand years.

"The tropical oceans are the driving mechanism of the climate," says climatologist Eric J. Barron of Pennsylvania State University. "The oceans are the memory of the climate system," adds Kirk Bryan of GFDL at Princeton. Yet until recently even the most advanced mathematical models treated the oceans only as vast, shallow swamps.

Carbon dioxide is absorbed by seawater, some of it incorporated into the shells of tiny marine creatures that die and become carbonate sediments on the bottom. Scientists estimate that a significant part of the seven billion metric tons of carbon released into the air each year is taken up in the seas. Oddly, the colder the water, the more CO_2 it can hold. As the oceans warm under the effect of more CO_2 in the atmosphere, there is great uncertainty about how much of that new CO_2 will be absorbed. Is there a limit to how much carbon can be locked away? Have the oceans already reached their holding capacity?

World-famed geochemist Wallace S. Broecker of Columbia University's Lamont-Doherty Geological Observatory worries that rapid switches in ocean circulation might occur under relatively small changes in global climate. Ice and seafloor core samples show that there have been sudden climate changes in the past, he says, from warming conditions to marked glaciation and back in as little time as a century. It could happen again.

As the seas and air warm, more water evaporates into the atmosphere, creating more clouds and another great enigma to the mathematical modelers. Much is yet unknown about the net effects of clouds on global weather.

"Clouds are the window shades of the planet," says Steve Schneider of NCAR. "They may be even more important than the oceans or the greenhouse gases in regulating the heat received from the sun."

In daylight low thick clouds reflect sunlight back into space and have a cooling effect. At night they hold in heat radiated from the surface and thus warm the atmosphere. High thin clouds, such as cirrus, may act differently, also adding to the greenhouse effect. Storm clouds transport and release vast amounts of heat.

The incredibly complicated interactions of the atmosphere, land, and oceans lead many scientists to doubt that local and regional weather patterns can ever be accurately predicted for more than a few days into the future. Listening to atmospheric (Continued on page 22)

Earthmovers replaced tugboats on the Mississippi River in 1988, as drought brought record low water that grounded barges near Memphis. The drought slashed U.S. corn production 30 percent, boosting the volume of futures trading at the Chicago Board of Trade. Wichita farmer Larry Steckline and son Greg lost $80,000 of wheat. Many scientists believe that while it didn't directly cause this devastation, global warming will make droughts and storms more frequent and severe.

(Continued from page 19) physicists discuss the new mathematical science called chaos is a form of mental mugging; they speak of random walks, strange attractors, and climatic ripples such as the "butterfly effect"—the notion put forward by MIT meteorologist Edward Lorenz that the flap of a butterfly's wings in Peru could lead to a tornado in Kansas. Yet these are today's frontiers of understanding.

The limit of that understanding leads Eric Barron of Penn State to quote Mark Twain's famous droll remark: "The researches of many commentators have already thrown much darkness on this subject, and it is probable that, if they continue, we shall soon know nothing at all about it."

Feedbacks—the relationships between the natural forces that control climate—will be the crucial key, most modelers agree: clouds affecting surface temperatures; rainfall and droughts changing soil moisture, vegetation, and evaporation; snow and ice melting from ice caps and glaciers, changing the reflectivity of the planet and raising the level of the seas.

More volcanic eruptions, throwing fine dust and gases high into the stratosphere, might operate against the greenhouse, cooling the earth temporarily. But the best computer models suggest that to bring on marked cooling, volcanic explosions far more violent than those of Mount St. Helens in 1980 or Krakatoa in 1883 would have to occur every five years for as long as a century. The resulting dirty air and acid rain would be worse for life on earth than global warming.

If a return to ice-age conditions rather than greenhouse warming sounds farfetched, it was thought a serious possibility as recently as the mid-1970s. The nine major interglacial periods

Clouds are the window shades of the planet. They may be even more important than the oceans or the greenhouse gases in regulating the heat received from the sun.

of the past million years have each lasted scarcely 10,000 years before the cold returned—and it has now been longer than that since the last great continental ice sheets melted back. And even though global temperature has been rising since the start of the industrial age, from 1940 until 1970 it leveled and even declined slightly in the Northern Hemisphere.

J. Murray Mitchell, Jr., senior climate researcher of the U. S. Weather Bureau and later of NOAA's Environmental Data Service, was one of those who documented that downward drift. Now retired, he told me recently: "We thought natural forces, such as volcanic activity or perhaps variation in the sun's radiance, might be at work. But we still don't know whether it was a real change or just a quarter-century-long twitch in the climate cycle."

Does the sun blaze absolutely uniformly, sending always the same amount of light, heat, and other radiation into space? Is its total radiance constant, as has long been assumed, or does the energy received by the earth vary, even minutely? The question is crucial in today's climate studies.

From astrophysical evidence the sun is thought to have been 25 to 30 percent dimmer when the earth was young—three and a half billion years ago. Pondering how life could have developed under this "faint young sun," earth scientists postulate that a super-greenhouse effect must have been at work, with 100 to 1,000 times as much CO_2 in the atmosphere. Otherwise the surface of the planet would have been frozen solid, and photosynthesis impossible. Yet it indeed occurred, absorbing much of the carbon dioxide and producing the oxygen in the atmosphere necessary for the evolution of life.

In the time of modern science the sun's radiation has seemed absolutely steady. Astronomers have tried for more than a century to detect any change in the "solar constant." It was only in the past decade that they succeeded.

The answer lay in taking solar instruments above the unsteady window of earth's atmosphere, into the black clarity of space. That goal was reached in February 1980 with the launch of the Solar Maximum Mission (SMM) satellite, dubbed Solar Max. It went into space to read solar output just as the number of sunspots—the dark areas on the sun's face that signal changes in its magnetic activity—had reached a peak in their 11-year cycle.

By 1985 Solar Max showed a real, though very slight, decline in the sun's brightness. The drop was only about one-tenth of one percent, but to solar physicists such as Richard Willson of the Jet Propulsion Laboratory, a principal scientist of the project, it was startling. If there is an actual fluctuation of the sun's output of even that small amount, it might have a long-term, measurable effect on global weather.

In 1986 the number of sunspots reached a minimum, as predicted. Shortly after, there began a rapid increase in sun-spots—greater than in any previous solar cycle of this century. Scientists expected the upturn to continue until the next peak in 1990 or '91, but an unforeseen hazard put the Solar Max project in peril.

As the sun's activity increased, it warmed the outermost fringe of earth's atmosphere slightly, causing it to expand. The added drag began to slow the satellite, and it dropped in its orbit by a few kilometers. Instead of circling the planet at least until 1991, Solar Max began tumbling in August 1989, and by early December ended its life as a fireball of blazing metal in the sky.

"Even without the Solar Max readings—long before this century, in fact—we've known that changes occur in the sun," I heard from John A. Eddy of the Office for Interdisciplinary Earth Studies in Boulder. He is one of the world's leading solar historians.

"Chinese, Korean, and Japanese court astronomers recorded spots on the sun at least 2,000 years ago. Galileo saw them in his first telescope in 1610. The fact that the spots varied on a regular cycle wasn't recognized until 1843, by a German amateur astronomer, Heinrich Schwabe. Their number and position changed, and in some years there were more of them, in other years and decades, many fewer.

"We know today," Jack Eddy went on, "that the spots not only are real but also indicate massive changes going on in the sun. As the spots cross its face—moving with the rotating body-they affect the total energy the sun sends out into space."

As outward evidence of magnetic disturbances on the sun, the spots sometimes herald solar storms or flares, which can disrupt short-wave radio communications on earth or with satellites and cause destructive surges in high-voltage power networks. In March 1989 a massive solar flare disrupted the electric-power grid of much of eastern Canada and produced spectacular shimmering lights in the ionosphere. The pulsating red, green, and white curtains called the aurora borealis, or northern lights, were seen as far south as Florida and Texas.

Do sunspots affect the planet's weather and climate? There have been times in past centuries when sunspots were very scarce—or missing entirely, if lack of any record of them can be believed. One notable

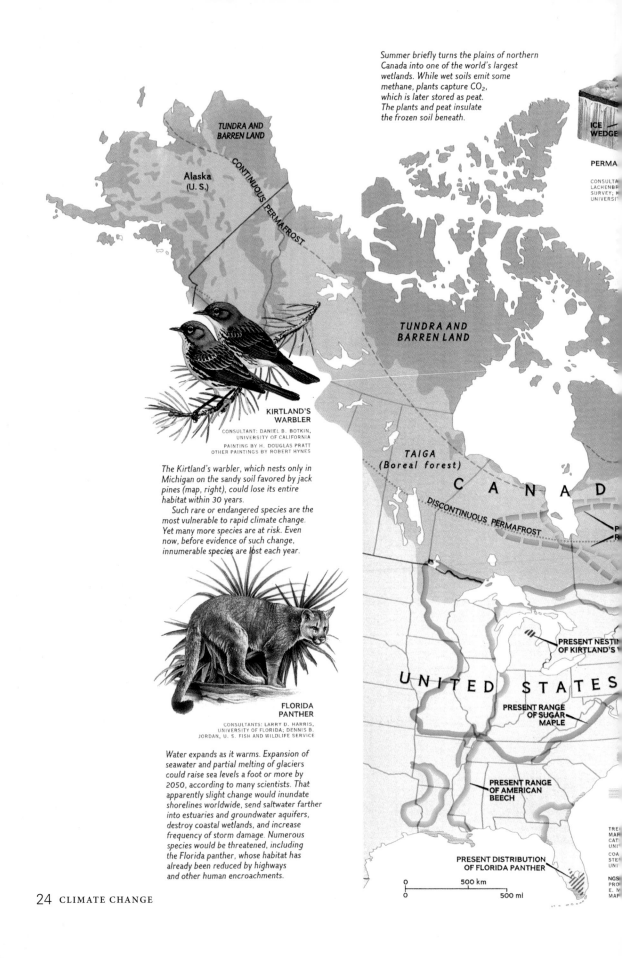

Summer briefly turns the plains of northern Canada into one of the world's largest wetlands. While wet soils emit some methane, plants capture CO_2, which is later stored as peat. The plants and peat insulate the frozen soil beneath.

ICE WEDGE

PERMA

CONSULTA
LACHENBR
SURVEY; M
UNIVERSI

TUNDRA AND BARREN LAND

Alaska (U. S.)

CONTINUOUS PERMAFROST

TUNDRA AND BARREN LAND

TAIGA (Boreal forest)

C A N A D

DISCONTINUOUS PERMAFROST

P
R

KIRTLAND'S WARBLER

CONSULTANT: DANIEL B. BOTKIN, UNIVERSITY OF CALIFORNIA

PAINTING BY H. DOUGLAS PRATT
OTHER PAINTINGS BY ROBERT HYNES

The Kirtland's warbler, which nests only in Michigan on the sandy soil favored by jack pines (map, right), could lose its entire habitat within 30 years.

Such rare or endangered species are the most vulnerable to rapid climate change. Yet many more species are at risk. Even now, before evidence of such change, innumerable species are lost each year.

PRESENT NESTI
OF KIRTLAND'S

U N I T E D   S T A T E S

PRESENT RANGE OF SUGAR MAPLE

FLORIDA PANTHER

CONSULTANTS: LARRY D. HARRIS, UNIVERSITY OF FLORIDA; DENNIS B. JORDAN, U. S. FISH AND WILDLIFE SERVICE

PRESENT RANGE OF AMERICAN BEECH

Water expands as it warms. Expansion of seawater and partial melting of glaciers could raise sea levels a foot or more by 2050, according to many scientists. That apparently slight change would inundate shorelines worldwide, send saltwater farther into estuaries and groundwater aquifers, destroy coastal wetlands, and increase frequency of storm damage. Numerous species would be threatened, including the Florida panther, whose habitat has already been reduced by highways and other human encroachments.

TRE
MA
CAT
UNI

COA
STE
UNI

PRESENT DISTRIBUTION OF FLORIDA PANTHER

NGS
PRO
E. M
MAP

0   500 km
0   500 mi

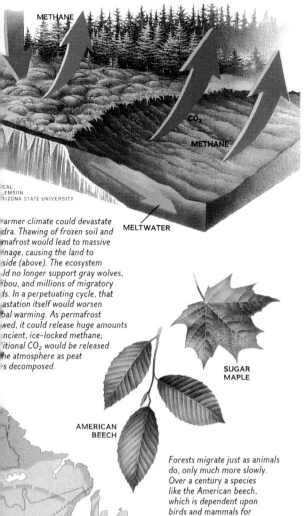

METHANE

CO₂

METHANE

CAL
...EMSON
...RIZONA STATE UNIVERSITY

MELTWATER

...armer climate could devastate
...dra. Thawing of frozen soil and
...mafrost would lead to massive
...nage, causing the land to
...side (above). The ecosystem
...ld no longer support gray wolves,
...ibou, and millions of migratory
...ds. In a perpetuating cycle, that
...astation itself would worsen
...bal warming. As permafrost
...wed, it could release huge amounts
...ncient, ice-locked methane;
...litional CO₂ would be released
...he atmosphere as peat
...s decomposed.

SUGAR
MAPLE

AMERICAN
BEECH

Forests migrate just as animals
do, only much more slowly.
Over a century a species
like the American beech,
which is dependent upon
birds and mammals for
dispersing its seeds, can
advance perhaps 20 miles.
Yet by then its range —
defined by temperature and
soil moisture — will have shifted
hundreds of miles to the north,
according to some warming
predictions (map, left). Beech
trees could virtually disappear
in the U. S. Sugar maples,
valued for furniture and
foliage as well as syrup, may
face the same fate.

Preview of a crisis

WARMER CONDITIONS than any felt
in the past 100,000 years will confront plants and animals if the
earth warms by 3°C by 2050, as some climatologists predict. Such a climate
change would be ten times faster than
any since the last ice age, hugely stressing
the web of life. Soil moisture patterns
could shift radically, as could relationships between predators and prey.

period was between 1645 and 1715, the
so-called Maunder Minimum, named for a
British solar astronomer of the 19th century.
The coincidence of their absence with the
particularly cold period of the Little Ice Age,
which gripped Europe from the 1400s to the
1800s, has long intrigued solar scientists.

Eddy and other astrophysicists point to the
Maunder and a sequence of earlier minimums
as the clearest evidence of long-term change in
the sun's total activity, perhaps in cycles longer
than the principal periods of 11 and 22 years,
and of a possible connection between sunspots and the earth's climate.

The evidence remains circumstantial. "But
there can be little doubt," Eddy has written,
"that variability is a real feature of the sun. The
challenge now is to understand it."

One clue to sunspots and their effects on
the earth lies in an unlikely repository—
the record of weather changes locked in the
growth rings of trees. At the Laboratory of
Tree-Ring Research of the University of Ari-
zona at Tucson, director Malcolm Hughes
and others showed me the 8,500-year con-
secutive tree-ring record acquired by that
pioneering laboratory in decades of work
in the U. S. Southwest. Periods of faster and
slower growth in tree rings since the 17th
century have been linked to wet periods and
droughts—and possibly to the sunspot cycle.

"There is clear variability in much of this
tree-ring record, in a pulse close to 20 years,"
Hughes said. "Scientists such as Murray
Mitchell and my colleague Charles Stockton
see this pulse as a combination of the sunspot
cycle and a lunar cycle of 18.6 years and relate
it to cyclical droughts in the West, such as the
1930s Dust Bowl.

"More than that, varying amounts of a carbon isotope in the tree rings—carbon 14—
may be a clue to long-term changes in solar
radiation and its effect on the earth's atmosphere," Hughes told me.

"The irregularities in the carbon-14 production rate are known as the Suess wiggles,

E

...ANTS:

...A

...ULTANT:
...S

...ON
...NDSMAN, JAMES
...HELLE H. PICARD
...ZIS

for Hans E. Suess, their discoverer. They are extremely important in calibrating and correcting the carbon-14 calendar used to date ancient events from remnants of organic materials, such as ancient wood or bones."

Other theories of sunspot-climate relationships have come and gone, but no true "smoking gun" had been found—until the mid-1980s. Then a German atmospheric physicist, Karin Labitzke of the Free University of Berlin, together with Harry van Loon of NCAR in Boulder, published a remarkable fit between reversing winds in the stratosphere, polar air temperatures, and the sunspot cycle. If their discovery is confirmed, it will indicate a direct link between sunspots and the atmosphere of earth—a possibly crucial connection. The work has been cited as among the most significant now being pursued at NCAR.

One connection may be a better understanding of the ozone hole in the so-called polar vortex over Antarctica each winter, a giant whirlpool of stratospheric winds.

In the mid-1980s the world became suddenly aware that the protective ozone shield in the atmosphere was in danger—was, in fact, greatly depleted in a huge "hole" over the frozen wastes of Antarctica. The mysterious stuff called ozone, which until then was known to the public chiefly as an acrid, lung-burning element of smog in overcrowded cities, was being destroyed in the stratosphere by chemicals made and released in the 20th century by humans.

Ozone is a variant form of oxygen—the most life-sustaining gas of all. Under the intense ultraviolet bombardment from the sun at the upper reaches of the earth's atmosphere, normal two-atom molecules of oxygen are split into single atoms—O rather than O_2, in chemists' terms. Some of these single oxygen atoms rejoin with O_2 molecules to form ozone—O_3. The amount in the stratosphere is very scant, less than ten parts per million (at sea level the layer would be about as thick as a pane of window glass), but that layer is enough to stop most of the sun's dangerous ultraviolet rays from reaching the earth's surface, 10 to 30 miles below.

The possibility of ozone destruction by man-made chemicals had been predicted as early as 1974 by two farsighted researchers, F. Sherwood Rowland and Mario J. Molina, at the University of California at Irvine.

Certain industrial gases dubbed CFCs—chlorofluorocarbons—are so highly stable and inert that they do not react with other substances in nature. Thus they have long been used as the coolants in refrigerators and air conditioners, as the propellants in aerosol cans, in making foam-plastic objects such as coffee cups and fast-food containers, and as solvents for cleaning electronic circuit boards and computer chips. But there could be great danger, warned Rowland and Molina, when those same long-lived gases drift to the upper layers of the atmosphere.

In that same region where ozone is created by solar bombardment, the CFCs could break apart, they postulated, freeing chlorine atoms that could attack and destroy ozone molecules by the billions. If this were to deplete the ozone layer around the whole world, it would put all mankind at risk.

The hazard was judged serious enough for the United States to ban CFCs from aerosol cans in the late 1970s. But CFCs are still produced for other uses, and millions of tons more lie waiting to be freed from scrapped refrigerators and air conditioners.

Then came the first startling report by British scientists in 1985 of an Antarctic ozone hole, and a rash of scare stories blossomed in the world's press. Emergency field studies of the stratosphere above Antarctica were mounted by U.S. science agencies, led by NASA, NOAA, and the National Science

Foundation. In 1987 an ER-2 aircraft, capable of flying to 70,000 feet in the stratosphere, and a DC-8 jammed with instruments flew from Punta Arenas, Chile, near the tip of South America, out across the ice-locked Antarctic continent.

The hole was real; the ozone had dropped by 50 percent.

The hole was real; the ozone had dropped by 50 percent. Its destruction was confined within the rotating swirl of winds in the polar vortex. And it was caused by a chemical reaction, not some unfathomed atmospheric phenomenon. The reaction seemed to occur in the presence of thin polar ice clouds that form in the intense cold of late winter, just before the sun returns to strike the polar latitudes.

Less than a year later, in September 1987, more than 40 nations sent delegates to Montreal, Canada. The industrialized countries agreed to reduce production of CFCs by 50 percent by 1998. A June 1990 revision called for a 100 percent ban by the year 2000, with a ten-year time lag for less developed nations.

Does another ozone hole develop over the Arctic in its winter? If the Northern Hemisphere, far more populous than the Southern, is also being depleted of its ozone umbrella, it might pose a far more serious emergency.

The same team of atmospheric scientists and computer experts, including Robert Watson of NASA and Adrian Tuck and Susan Solomon of NOAA, spent 45 cold, bleak days in January and February 1989 in the North Sea port of Stavanger, Norway. There the same ER-2 and DC-8 flew 28 missions, from the northernmost airstrip that could safely be used, to take readings from the air of the polar Arctic.

It took a year to analyze all the data. In March 1990 the scientists published their answer. The polar vortex and ice clouds existed also in the northern stratosphere, though not to the same extent as in the southern. Ozone was being depleted in the Arctic as well, by as much as 15 to 17 percent at some altitudes.

Over the heavily populated mid-latitudes of the globe, the researchers believe, winter ozone levels may have dropped in the past decade by as much as 4 to 6 percent. And even if all CFC production worldwide were to be halted—an unlikely possibility even to the signers of the Montreal Protocol—the amount already existing and waiting to be released to the atmosphere would mean a continuing ozone drop for decades to come.

The worry is that stratospheric ozone forms the earth's principal shield against dangerous ultraviolet radiation from the sun. This short wavelength light, below the range of human visibility, kills many forms of life—bacteria, for example, which is why it is used for sterilizing surgical instruments and protecting many foods. But ultraviolet also kills beneficial forms of life, and it can affect the life cycle of many plants, both on land and in the seas.

Middle and long wavelengths of UV cause not just tanning and extreme sunburn in human skin but the most prevalent forms of skin cancer. They also can cause cataracts in the eyes and injure the immune responses of skin, which protect us from many harmful, even deadly diseases.

The Environmental Protection Agency issued a risk assessment in 1987, predicting that for every one percent drop in global ozone, there would be a one to three percent increase in skin cancers. Global ozone has dropped at least 2 percent in the past ten years, EPA said, leading to possibly four million added cases of skin cancer. In the past ten years alone, dangerous skin.

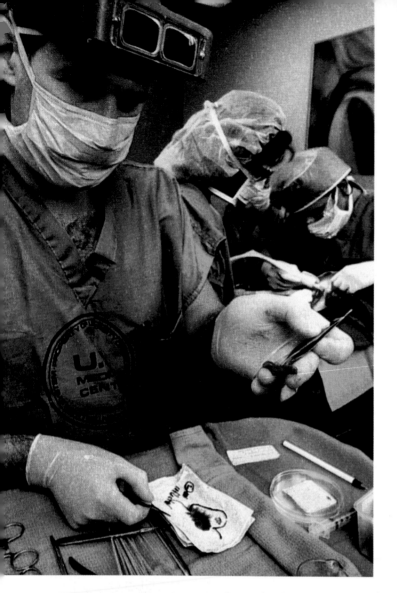

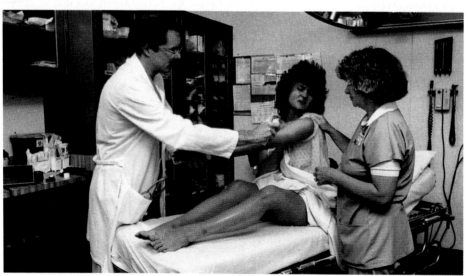

"Mad dogs and Englishmen go out in the midday sun," wrote playwright Noël Coward. *But they pay a price. More than 60 percent of the sun's ultraviolet light (UV) strikes between 10 a.m. and 3 p.m., increasing the risk of tissue damage. A Memorial Day visit to Virginia Beach sent Sue Polinsky to the hospital with first-degree burns (bottom left). UV's cumulative effects can cause both fatal and non-fatal skin cancers, which are fast increasing in the U.S. Dr. Roy Grekin of the University of California, San Francisco, holds a tumor he just removed from a patient's ear (top left).*

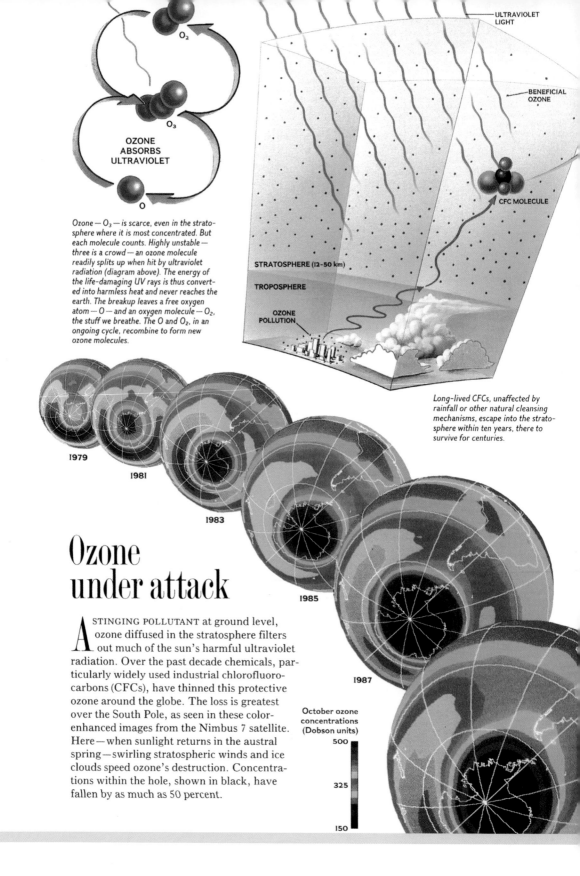

O₂

OZONE ABSORBS ULTRAVIOLET

O₃

O

ULTRAVIOLET LIGHT

BENEFICIAL OZONE

CFC MOLECULE

STRATOSPHERE (12-50 km)

TROPOSPHERE

OZONE POLLUTION

Ozone — O₃ — is scarce, even in the stratosphere where it is most concentrated. But each molecule counts. Highly unstable — three is a crowd — an ozone molecule readily splits up when hit by ultraviolet radiation (diagram above). The energy of the life-damaging UV rays is thus converted into harmless heat and never reaches the earth. The breakup leaves a free oxygen atom — O — and an oxygen molecule — O₂, the stuff we breathe. The O and O₂, in an ongoing cycle, recombine to form new ozone molecules.

Long-lived CFCs, unaffected by rainfall or other natural cleansing mechanisms, escape into the stratosphere within ten years, there to survive for centuries.

1979

1981

1983

Ozone under attack

A STINGING POLLUTANT at ground level, ozone diffused in the stratosphere filters out much of the sun's harmful ultraviolet radiation. Over the past decade chemicals, particularly widely used industrial chlorofluorocarbons (CFCs), have thinned this protective ozone around the globe. The loss is greatest over the South Pole, as seen in these color-enhanced images from the Nimbus 7 satellite. Here — when sunlight returns in the austral spring — swirling stratospheric winds and ice clouds speed ozone's destruction. Concentrations within the hole, shown in black, have fallen by as much as 50 percent.

1985

1987

October ozone concentrations (Dobson units)

500

325

150

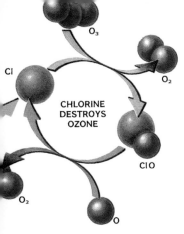

O₃

Cl

CHLORINE
DESTROYS
OZONE

O₂

ClO

O₂

O

When a UV ray strikes a CFC molecule, it
releases a chlorine atom — Cl — which then
attacks ozone molecules in a catalytic
reaction (above). The chlorine breaks the
ozone — O_3 — into ordinary oxygen —
O_2 — and combines with the free atom of
oxygen to form chlorine monoxide — ClO.
This is then stripped of its oxygen atom
by another free oxygen atom that joins it
to become ordinary oxygen. The chlorine
atom is left intact to repeat its destruction.
It may do so 100,000 times before it is
finally neutralized.

PAINTING BY MARK SEIDLER
OZONE CONSULTANT: MARK R. SCHOEBERL,
NASA/GODDARD SPACE FLIGHT CENTER (GSFC)
CHEMISTRY CONSULTANT: MARTIN R.
FELDMAN, HOWARD UNIVERSITY

TOTAL OZONE MAPPING SPECTROMETER IMAGES
PROVIDED BY NASA/GSFC

Propelled by energetic winds and one of the world's strongest economies, California produces 85 percent of the planet's wind-generated power. The state's 17,000 wind turbines, like these in Altamont Pass (top), provide enough electricity—about one percent of the yearly total—to meet all the residential needs of a city the size of nearby San Francisco. Experts say wind power could eventually produce 10 percent of the United States energy supply.

Another 10 percent of the supply could come from solar energy, including photo-voltaic cells. Today such cells power everything from calculators and demonstration cars to remote telecommunications stations and water pumps.

Discussion Questions

- At the time of this article (1990), what was the level of CO_2 in the atmosphere in parts per million, and how had it changed? How is it measured and how regularly (at what intervals)?

- Describe the green house effect, and how it influences the climate on earth.

- Discuss some predicted effects of climate change.

- Describe the state of climate modeling in 1990 and discuss its successes and limitations.

- Describe the role oceans play in the cycling of carbon dioxide in the atmosphere.

- What are the three points on which most climatologists agree regarding climate change circa 1990?

Challenges and Solutions

Identify one or more consequences of climate change, and indicate how it might influence you in your local environment. Propose two or three possible solutions to this issue and build an argument for the best, most realistic and socially acceptable solution.

Social Implications

Identify the social implications of climate change and how various stakeholders or interest groups might be affected (e.g. people living in low-lying coastal environments, or surfers in the southern hemisphere who are exposed to high levels of UV radiation). Choose one of these groups and explore their perspective. Assume that this group is taking their issue to the annual global climate change summit, and they wish to issue a press release about their issues and concerns. Write that press release and either a) submit it as a paper, b) give a group presentation to the course, or c) post it to the course blog as directed by your instructor.

SAVING ENERGY:
IT STARTS AT HOME

There are many approaches to addressing the climate change issue. The one that is most accessible to individuals on a daily basis is taking control of energy use and making conscious decisions to increase efficiency and reduce consumption. The following article explores this approach from the perspective of individuals engaging in an experiment to see if the reduction of carbon emissions is really possible for everyday people. Their results indicate that there are challenges and drawbacks, but ultimately, it can be done.

**As you read "Saving Energy: It Starts at Home,"
consider the following questions:**

- How much do carbon emissions need to be reduced in order to avoid the catastrophic melting of the world's ice sheets?

- What are some ways of reducing energy consumption in the home?

- What portion of the world's carbon dioxide emissions is produced by the United States?

- What are the three major sources of carbon dioxide emissions?

- The article argues that with little investment, it is within the capacity of any individual to reduce energy consumption by at least 25%. What factors are hindering people from doing so?

Thermographic photography offers clues to where energy is being wasted in this older house in Connecticut. Red and yellow patches indicate escaping heat, while new double-pane windows appear cool blue. By sealing in warmth, the windows cut heating costs, which can account for up to half a family's energy bill.

SAVING ENERGY: IT STARTS AT HOME

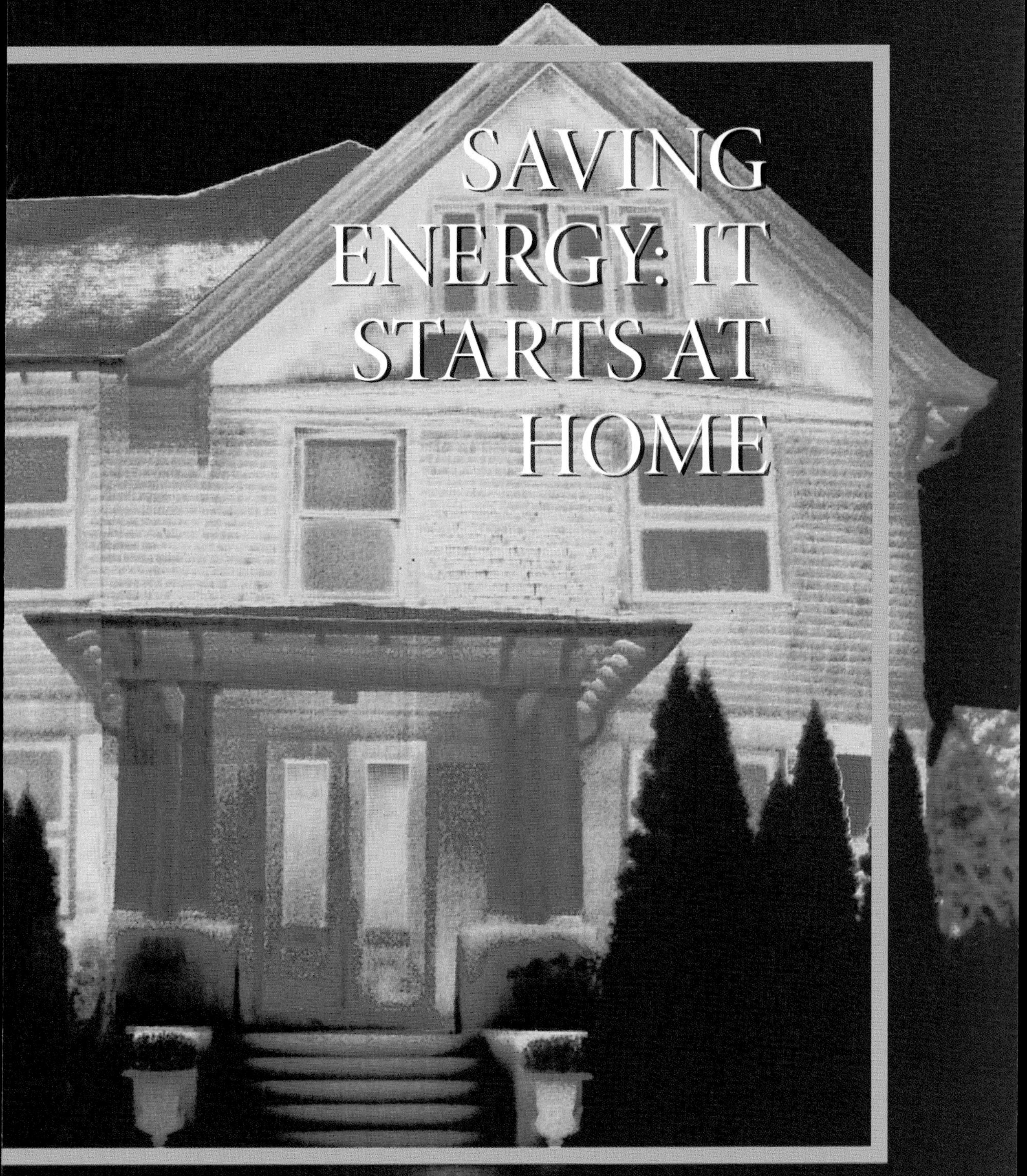

By Peter Miller

Photographs by Tyrone Turner

"We're farm people," says Janice Haney of Greensburg, Kansas.
"I enjoy hanging clothes out. We don't have to waste electricity
on the dryer. The good old Kansas wind can do it on its own."

WE ALREADY KNOW THE FASTEST, LEAST EXPENSIVE WAY TO SLOW CLIMATE CHANGE: USE LESS ENERGY.

WITH A LITTLE EFFORT, AND NOT MUCH MONEY,

MOST OF US COULD REDUCE OUR ENERGY DIETS BY 25 PERCENT OR MORE—DOING THE EARTH A FAVOR WHILE ALSO HELPING OUR POCKETBOOKS. SO WHAT'S HOLDING US BACK?

How close could we come to a lifestyle the planet could handle?

Not long ago, my wife, PJ, and I tried a new diet—not to lose a little weight but to answer a nagging question about climate change. Scientists have reported recently that the world is heating up even faster than predicted only a few years ago, and that the consequences could be severe if we don't keep reducing emissions of carbon dioxide and other greenhouse gases that are trapping heat in our atmosphere. But what can we do about it as individuals? And as emissions from China, India, and other developing nations skyrocket, will our efforts really make any difference?

We decided to try an experiment. For one month we tracked our personal emissions of carbon dioxide (CO_2) as if we were counting calories. We wanted to see how much we could cut back, so we put ourselves on a strict diet. The average U.S. household produces about 150 pounds of CO_2 a day by doing commonplace things like turning on air-conditioning or driving cars. That's more than twice the European average and almost five times the global average, mostly because Americans drive more and have bigger houses. But how much should we try to reduce?

For an answer, I checked with Tim Flannery, author of The Weather Makers: How Man Is Changing the Climate and What It Means for Life on Earth. In his book, he'd challenged readers to make deep cuts in personal emissions to keep the world from reaching critical tipping points, such as the melting of the ice sheets in Greenland or West Antarctica. "To stay below that threshold, we need to reduce CO_2 emissions by 80 percent," he said.

"That sounds like a lot," PJ said. "Can we really do that?"

It seemed unlikely to me too. Still, the point was to answer a simple question: How close could we come to a lifestyle the planet could handle? If it turned out we couldn't do it, perhaps we could at least identify places where the diet pinched and figure out ways to adjust. So we agreed to shoot for 80 percent less than the U.S. average, which equated to a daily diet of only 30 pounds of CO_2. Then we set out to find a few neighbors to join us. (Continued on page 41)

Adapted from "Saving Energy: It Starts at Home" by Peter Miller: National Geographic Magazine, March 2009.

THE MISSING POWER PLANT
Instead of building a new 730-megawatt facility like the Decker Power Plant, the Austin, Texas, electric utility reduced demand by the same amount through rebates on energy-saving appliances and other programs. "Go into any store in Austin, and you can't buy an inefficient air conditioner," says general manager Roger Duncan. "They just stopped stocking them."

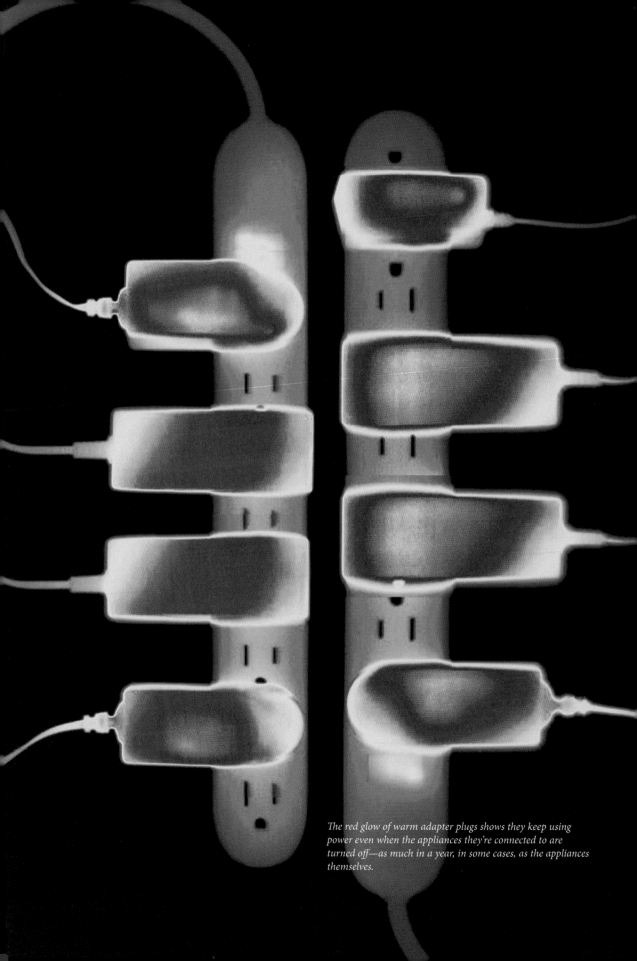

The red glow of warm adapter plugs shows they keep using power even when the appliances they're connected to are turned off—as much in a year, in some cases, as the appliances themselves.

(Continued from page 37) John and Kyoko Bauer were logical candidates. Dedicated greenies, they were already committed to a low-impact lifestyle. One car, one TV, no meat except fish. As parents of three-year-old twins, they were also worried about the future. "Absolutely, sign us up," John said.

Susan and Mitch Freedman, meanwhile, had two teenagers. Susan wasn't sure how eager they would be to cut back during their summer vacation, but she was game to give the diet a try. As an architect, Mitch was working on an office building designed to be energy efficient, so he was curious how much they could save at home. So the Freedmans were in too.

We started on a Sunday in July, an unseasonably mild day in Northern Virginia, where we live. A front had blown through the night before, and I'd opened our bedroom windows to let in the breeze. We'd gotten so used to keeping our air-conditioning going around the clock, I'd almost forgotten the windows even opened. The birds woke us at five with a pleasant racket in the trees, the sun came up, and our experiment began.

Our first challenge was to find ways to convert our daily activities into pounds of CO_2. We wanted to track our progress as we went, to change our habits if necessary.

PJ volunteered to read our electric meter each morning and to check the odometer on our Mazda Miata. While she was doing that, I wrote down the mileage from our Honda CR-V and pushed my way through the shrubs to read the natural gas meter. We diligently recorded everything on a chart taped to one of our kitchen cabinets. A gallon of gasoline, we learned, adds a whopping 19.6 pounds of CO_2 to the atmosphere, a big chunk of our daily allowance. A kilowatt-hour (kWh) of electricity in the U.S. produces 1.5 pounds of CO_2. Every 100 cubic feet of natural gas emits 12 pounds of CO_2.

To get a rough idea of our current carbon footprint, I plugged numbers from recent utility bills into several calculators on websites.

THE POWERED HOUSE

Electricity is the biggest source of power for U.S. homes—and for every kilowatt-hour used, 2.2 are "lost" as that energy is generated and sent over transmission lines. So, even small changes in our habits can scale up to big reductions in carbon emissions.

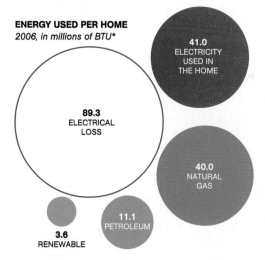

ENERGY USED PER HOME
2006, in millions of BTU*

89.3 ELECTRICAL LOSS

41.0 ELECTRICITY USED IN THE HOME

40.0 NATURAL GAS

11.1 PETROLEUM

3.6 RENEWABLE

If we converted half of all light-bulbs to compact fluorescents, we would reduce CO_2 from lighting by 42.4 million tons a year, or 36 percent.

If we turned off home computers when not in use, we would cut their CO_2 impact by 8.3 million tons a year, or 50 percent.

CO_2 AMOUNTS MEASURED IN METRIC TONS

*THE BRITISH THERMAL UNIT (BTU) IS USED TO MEASURE THE ENERGY CONTENT OF FUELS AND THE POWER OF HEATING AND COOLING SYSTEMS. ONE KILOWATT-HOUR OF ELECTRICITY IS EQUIVALENT TO 3,412 BTU.

SEAN MCNAUGHTON, NG STAFF

SOURCE: ENERGY INFORMATION ADMINISTRATION, ANNUAL ENERGY OUTLOOK 2008

Each asked for slightly different information, and each came up with a different result. None was flattering. The Environmental Protection Agency (EPA) website figured our annual CO_2 emissions at 54,273 pounds, 30 percent higher than the average American family with two people; the main culprit was the energy we were using to heat and cool our house. Evidently, we had further to go than I thought.

I began our campaign by grabbing a flashlight and heading down to the basement. For most families, the water heater alone consumes 12 percent of their house's energy. My plan was to turn down the heater's thermostat to 120°F, as experts recommend. But taking a close look at our tank, I saw only "hot" and "warm" settings, no degrees. Not knowing what that meant exactly, I twisted the dial to warm and hoped for the best. (The water turned out to be a little cool, and I had to adjust it later.)

When PJ drove off in the CR-V to pick up a friend for church, I hauled out gear to cut the grass: electric lawn mower, electric edger, electric leaf blower. Then it dawned on me: All this power-sucking equipment was going to cost us in CO_2 emissions. So I stuffed everything back into the garage, hopped in the Miata, and buzzed down the street to Home Depot to price out an old-fashioned push reel mower.

The store didn't have one, so I drove a few miles more to Lawn & Leisure, an outfit that specializes in lawn mowers. They were out too, though they had plenty of big riding mowers on display. (The average gasoline-powered push mower, I'd learned, puts out as much pollution per hour as eleven cars—a riding mower as much as 34 cars.) My next stop was Wal-Mart, where I found another empty spot on the rack. I finally tried Sears, which had one manual mower left, the display model.

I'd seen advertisements for the latest reel mowers that made them sound like precision instruments, not the clunky beast I pushed as a teenager. But when I gave the display model a spin across the sales floor, I was disappointed. The reel felt clumsy compared with my corded electric model, which I can easily maneuver with one hand. I got back in the car empty-handed and drove home.

As I pulled into the driveway, I had the sinking realization I'd been off on a fool's errand. I didn't know exactly how foolish until the next morning, when we added up the numbers. I'd driven 24 miles in search of a more Earth-friendly mower. PJ had driven

I didn't realize how foolish I was until the next morning: I'd driven 24 miles in search of a more Earth-friendly lawn mower.

27 miles to visit a friend in an assisted-living facility. We'd used 32 kWh of electricity and 100 cubic feet of gas to cook dinner and dry our clothes. Our total CO_2 emissions for the day: 105.6 pounds. Three and a half times our target.

"Guess we need to try harder," PJ said.

We got some help in week two from a professional "house doctor," Ed Minch, of Energy Services Group in Wilmington, Delaware. We asked Minch to do an energy audit of our house to see if we'd missed any easy fixes. The first thing he did was walk around the outside of the house, looking at how the "envelope" was put together. Had the architect and builder created any opportunities for air to seep in or out, such as overhanging floors? Next he went inside and used an infrared scanner to look at our interior walls. A hot or cold spot might mean that we had a duct problem or that insulation in a wall wasn't doing its job. Finally his assistants set up a powerful fan in our front door to lower air pressure inside the house and force air through whatever leaks there might be in the shell of the house. Our house, his instruments showed, was 50 percent leakier than it should be.

One reason, Minch discovered, was that our builder had left a narrow, rectangular hole in our foundation beneath the laundry room— for what reason we could only guess. Leaves from our yard had blown through the hole into the crawl space. "There's your big hit," he said. "That's your open window." I hadn't looked inside the crawl space in years, so there could have been a family of monkeys under there for all I knew. Sealing up that hole was now a priority, since heating represents up to half of a house's energy costs, and cooling can account for a tenth.

Air rushing in through the foundation was only part of the problem, however. Much of

YOU GET TO READ THE PAPER TOO

Commuters on a Metrorail train contribute only half as much CO_2 to the atmosphere as drivers on the Beltway around Washington, D.C. For every mile on the road, an average American car—often carrying just one or two people—pumps a pound of CO_2 into the sky. Emissions from operating an electric train (mainly from coal-fired power plants) are spread among thousands of riders.

the rest was air seeping out of a closet on our second floor, where a small furnace unit was located. The closet had never been completely drywalled, so air filtered through insulation in the roof to the great outdoors. Minch recommended we finish the drywalling when the time comes to replace the furnace.

Minch also gave us tips about lighting and appliances. "A typical kitchen these days has ten 75-watt spots on all day," he said. "That's a huge waste of money." Replacing them with compact fluorescents could save a homeowner $200 a year. Refrigerators, washing machines, dishwashers, and other appliances, in fact, may represent half of a household's electric bill. Those with Energy Star labels from the EPA are more efficient and may come with rebates or tax credits when you buy them, Minch said.

There was no shortage of advice out there, I discovered, about ways to cut back on CO_2 emissions. Even before Minch's visit, I'd collected stacks of printouts and brochures from environmental websites and utility companies. In a sense, there's almost too much information.

"You can't fix everything at once," John Bauer said when I asked how he and Kyoko were getting along. "When we became vegetarians, we didn't do it all at once. First the lamb went. Then the pork. Then the beef. Finally the chicken. We've been phasing out seafood for a few years now. It's no different with a carbon diet."

Good advice, I'm sure. But everywhere I looked I saw things gobbling up energy. One night I sat up in bed, squinted into the

Today's internal combustion engines are inefficient at converting fuel to motion. Cars waste up to 85 percent of the energy from the fuel in their tanks, losing a big chunk as heat.

darkness, and counted ten little lights: cell phone charger, desktop calculator, laptop computer, printer, clock radio, cable TV box, camera battery recharger, carbon monoxide detector, cordless phone base, smoke detector. What were they all doing? A study by the Lawrence Berkeley National Laboratory found that "vampire" power sucked up by electronics in standby mode can add up to 8 percent of a house's electric bill. What else had I missed?

"You can go nuts thinking about everything in your house that uses power," said Jennifer Thorne Amann, author of Consumer Guide to Home Energy Savings, who had agreed to be our group's energy coach. "You have to use

common sense and prioritize. Don't agonize too much. Think about what you'll be able to sustain after the experiment is over. If you have trouble reaching your goal in one area, remember there's always something else you can do."

At this point we left home for a long weekend to attend the wedding of my niece, Alyssa, in Oregon. While we were gone, the house sitter caring for our two dogs continued to read our gas and electric meters, and we kept track of the mileage on our rental car as we drove from Portland to the Pacific coast. I knew this trip wasn't going to help our carbon diet any. But what was more important, after all, reducing CO_2 emissions or sharing a family celebration?

That's the big question. How significant are personal efforts to cut back? Do our actions add up to anything meaningful, or are we just making ourselves feel better? I still wasn't sure. As soon as we returned home to Virginia, I started digging up more numbers.

The United States, I learned, produces a fifth of the world's CO_2 emissions, about six billion metric tons a year. That staggering amount could reach seven billion by 2030, as our population and economy continue to grow. Most of the CO_2 comes from energy consumed by buildings, vehicles, and industries. How much CO_2 could be avoided, I started to wonder, if we all tightened our belts? What would happen if the whole country went on a carbon diet?

Buildings, not cars, produce the most CO_2 in the United States. Private residences, shopping malls, warehouses, and offices account for 38 percent of the nation's emissions, mainly because of electricity use. It doesn't help that the average new house in the United States is 45 percent bigger than it was 30 years ago.

Companies like Wal-Mart that maintain thousands of their own buildings have discovered they can achieve significant energy savings. A pilot Supercenter in Las Vegas consumes up to 45 percent less power than similar stores, in part by using evaporative cooling units, radiant floors, high-efficiency refrigeration, and natural light in shopping areas. Retrofits and smart design could reduce emissions from buildings in this country by 200 million tons of CO_2 a year, according to researchers at Oak Ridge National Laboratory. But Americans are unlikely to achieve such gains, they say, without new building codes, appliance standards, and financial incentives. There are simply too many reasons not to.

Commercial building owners, for example, have had little incentive to pay more for improvements like high-efficiency windows,

TRANSPORTATION TOLLS

Cars and light trucks consume the lion's share of petroleum used for transportation in the U.S. Modest changes in efficiency and driving habits could add up to significant fuel savings.

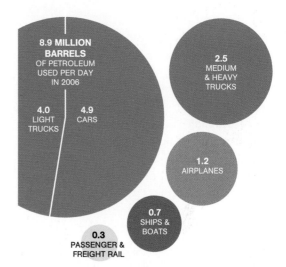

8.9 MILLION BARRELS OF PETROLEUM USED PER DAY IN 2006

4.0 LIGHT TRUCKS

4.9 CARS

2.5 MEDIUM & HEAVY TRUCKS

1.2 AIRPLANES

0.7 SHIPS & BOATS

0.3 PASSENGER & FREIGHT RAIL

If we drove our cars 20 fewer miles each week, we could reduce their CO_2 emissions by 107 million tons each year, a 9 percent decrease.

If we improved our cars' gas mileage by 5 miles a gallon, we could cut their CO_2 emissions by 239 million tons each year, a 20 percent decrease.

CO_2 AMOUNTS MEASURED IN METRIC TONS

SEAN MCNAUGHTON, NG STAFF

SOURCES: ENERGY INFORMATION ADMINISTRATION, ANNUAL ENERGY OUTLOOK 2008; DEPARTMENT OF ENERGY, TRANSPORTATION ENERGY DATA BOOK, EDITION 27

lights, heating, or cooling systems since their tenants, not they, pay the energy bills, said Harvey Sachs of the American Council for an Energy-Efficient Economy. For homeowners, meanwhile, efficiency takes a backseat whenever money is tight. In a 2007 survey of Americans, 60 percent said they didn't have enough savings to pay for energy-related renovations. If given an extra $10,000 to work with, only 24 percent said they would invest in efficiency. What did the rest want? Granite countertops.

After buildings, transportation is the next largest source of CO_2, producing 34 percent of the nation's emissions. Carmakers have been told by Congress to raise fuel economy standards by 40 percent by 2020. But emissions will still grow, because the number of miles driven in this country keeps going up. One big reason: Developers keep pushing neighborhoods farther into the countryside, making it unavoidable for families to spend hours a day in their cars. An EPA study estimated that greenhouse gas emissions from vehicles could increase 80 percent over the next 50 years. Unless we make it easier for Americans to choose buses, subways, and bikes over cars, experts say, there's little chance for big emissions cuts from vehicles.

The industrial sector represents the third major source of CO_2. Refineries, paper plants, and other facilities emit 28 percent of the nation's total. You would think such enterprises would have eliminated inefficiencies long ago. But that isn't always the case. For firms competing in global markets, making the best product at the right price comes first. Reducing greenhouse gases is less urgent. Some don't even track CO_2 emissions.

A number of corporations such as Dow, DuPont, and 3M have shown how profitable efficiency can be. Since 1995, Dow has saved seven billion dollars by reducing its energy intensity—the amount of energy consumed per pound of product—and during the past few decades it has cut its CO_2 emissions by 20 percent. To show other companies how to make such gains, the Department of Energy (DOE) has been sending teams of experts into 700 or so factories a year to analyze equipment and techniques. Yet even here change doesn't come easily. Managers are reluctant to invest in efficiency unless the return is high and the payback time is short. Even when tips from the experts involve no cost at all—such as "turn off the ventilation in unoccupied rooms"—fewer than half of such fixes are acted upon. One reason is inertia. "Many changes don't happen until the maintenance foreman, who

Buildings, not cars, produce the most CO_2 in the U.S. The average new house is 45 percent bigger than it was 30 years ago.

knows how to keep the old equipment running, dies or retires," said Peggy Podolak, senior industrial energy analyst at DOE.

But change is coming anyway. Most business leaders expect federal regulation of CO_2 emissions in the near future. Already, New York and nine other northeastern states have agreed on a mandatory cap-and-trade system similar to the one started in Europe in 2005. Under the plan, launched last year, emissions from large power plants will be reduced over time, as each plant either cuts emissions or purchases credits from other companies that cut their emissions. A similar scheme has been launched by the governors of California and six other western states and the premiers of four Canadian provinces.

So how do the numbers add up? How much CO_2 could we save if the whole nation went on a low carbon diet? A study by McKinsey & Company, a management consulting firm, estimated that the United States could avoid 1.3 billion tons of CO_2 emissions a year, using only existing technologies that would pay for themselves in savings. Instead of growing by more than a billion tons by 2020, annual emissions in the U.S. would drop by 200 million tons a year. We already know, in other words, how to freeze CO_2 emissions if we want to.

Not that there won't still be obstacles. Every sector of our economy faces challenges, said energy-efficiency guru Amory Lovins of the Rocky Mountain Institute. "But they all have huge potential. I don't know anyone who has failed to make money at energy efficiency. There's so much low-hanging fruit, it's falling off the trees and mushing up around our ankles."

By the last week in July, PJ and I were finally getting into the flow of the reduced carbon lifestyle. We walked to the neighborhood pool instead of driving, biked to the farmers market on Saturday morning, and lingered on

A GREEN DREAM HOUSE
After a monster tornado swept away their home in 2007, Jill and Scott Eller of Greensburg, Kansas, decided to rebuild using a more efficient design. Their new house, constructed from structural insulated panels like the one Jill is holding, is expected to be much more airtight than standard wood-frame houses. As a bonus, the domes should deflect all but the strongest of winds.

the deck until dark, chatting over the chirping of the crickets. Whenever possible I worked from home, and when I commuted I took the bus and subway. Even when it got hot and humid, as it does in Virginia in July, we were never really uncomfortable, thanks in part to the industrial-size ceiling fan we installed in the bedroom in late June.

"That fan's my new best friend," PJ said.

Our numbers were looking pretty good, in fact, when we crossed the finish line on August 1. Compared with the previous July, we slashed electricity use by 70 percent, natural gas by 40 percent, and reduced our driving to half the national average. In terms of CO_2, we trimmed our emissions to an average of 70.5 pounds a day, which, though twice as much as we'd targeted as our goal, was still half the national average.

These were encouraging results, I thought, until I factored in emissions from our plane trip to Oregon. I hadn't expected that a modern aircraft packed with passengers would emit almost half as much CO_2 per person as PJ and I would have produced if we'd driven to Oregon and back in the CR-V. The round-trip flight added the equivalent of 2,500 pounds of CO_2 to our bottom line, more than doubling our daily average from 70.5 pounds of CO_2 to 150 pounds—five times our goal. So much for air travel.

By comparison, the Bauers did significantly better, though they also faced setbacks. Since their house is all electric, Kyoko Bauer had tried to reduce her use of the clothes dryer by hanging laundry on a rack outside, as she and John had done when they lived in arid Western Australia. But with their (Continued on page 50)

BRINGING THE FARM TO THE CITY
If tomatoes, cucumbers, lettuce, strawberries, pumpkins, and other crops can grow on a barge in the Hudson River, then why not on New York City rooftops? That was the idea behind the Science Barge, a prototype of a carbon-neutral hydroponic farm that saves energy by eliminating the need for transportation.

DOING LESS HARM IN FLIGHT
Because aircraft exhaust is released at high altitude, scientists say it has a greater impact on climate than the same emissions at ground level. At a General Electric test site in Peebles, Ohio, technicians check connections before firing up a GEnx-2B development engine. Built with carbon-fiber parts, the test model uses less fuel and produces 15 percent less CO_2 than predecessors.

(Continued from page 47) busy three-year-olds, Etienne and Ajanta, she was doing as many as 14 loads a week, and it took all day for clothes to dry in Virginia's humid air. "It wasn't as convenient as I hoped," she said. "I had to race home from shopping a couple of times before it started to rain." Their bottom line: 97.4 pounds of CO_2 a day.

For the Freedmans, driving turned out to be the big bump in the road. With four cars and everyone commuting to a job every day—including Ben and Courtney—they racked up 4,536 miles during the month. "I don't know how we could have driven less," Susan said. "We were all going in different directions and there wasn't any other way to get there." Their bottom line: 248 pounds of CO_2 a day.

When we received our electric bill for July, PJ and I were pleased that our efforts had saved us $190. We decided to use a portion of this windfall to offset the airline emissions. After doing a little homework, we contributed $50 to Native Energy, one of many companies and nonprofits that save CO_2 by investing in wind farms, solar plants, and other renewable energy projects. Our purchase was enough to counteract a ton of jet emissions, roughly what we added through our trip and then some.

We can do more, of course. We can sign up with our utility company for power from regional wind farms. We can purchase locally grown foods instead of winter raspberries from Chile and bottled water from Fiji. We can join a carbon-reduction club through a neighborhood church, Scout troop, Rotary Club, PTA, or environmental group. If we can't find one, we could start one. (Continued on page 54)

Blue signifies the cool air escaping as four-year-old Eva Turner dawdles at the fridge. That's not so bad: Today's models use a third less energy than those of 30 years ago.

A CARBON REDUCTION PLAN

By investing in new technology or adopting approaches already available, we could cut U.S. greenhouse gas emissions by three billion tons a year, more than offsetting the increases expected by 2030 as our population and economy grow. And the money saved from efficiencies in how we use energy (below) could help pay for improvements in how we generate energy (right).

KEY SECTORS

1,127 million tons per year

729 million tons per year

520 million tons per year

486 million tons per year

357 million tons per year

CUTS THAT SAVE MONEY

About 40 percent of possible cuts could come from measures that save billions of dollars a year (below). Most of these savings are found in building improvements, such as more efficient lighting, and transportation improvements like better fuel efficiency.

CO_2 REDUCTIONS ▶ (IN BILLIONS OF TONS PER YEAR)

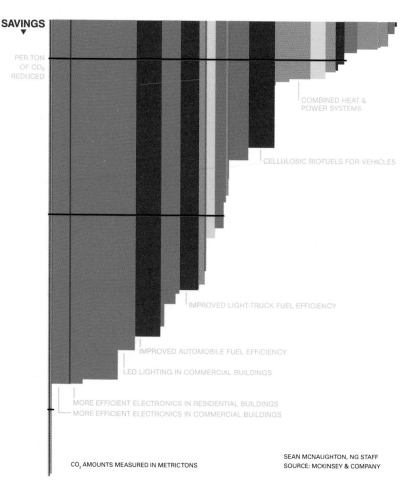

SAVINGS
▼

PER TON
OF CO_2
REDUCED

COMBINED HEAT &
POWER SYSTEMS

CELLULOSIC BIOFUELS FOR VEHICLES

IMPROVED LIGHT-TRUCK FUEL EFFICIENCY

IMPROVED AUTOMOBILE FUEL EFFICIENCY

LED LIGHTING IN COMMERCIAL BUILDINGS

MORE EFFICIENT ELECTRONICS IN RESIDENTIAL BUILDINGS
MORE EFFICIENT ELECTRONICS IN COMMERCIAL BUILDINGS

CO_2 AMOUNTS MEASURED IN METRIC TONS

SEAN MCNAUGHTON, NG STAFF
SOURCE: MCKINSEY & COMPANY

CUTS THAT COST MONEY

The power industry could achieve big carbon reductions by developing renewable energy and adopting measures such as carbon capture-and-storage for coal plants (below), though initial investments would be high.

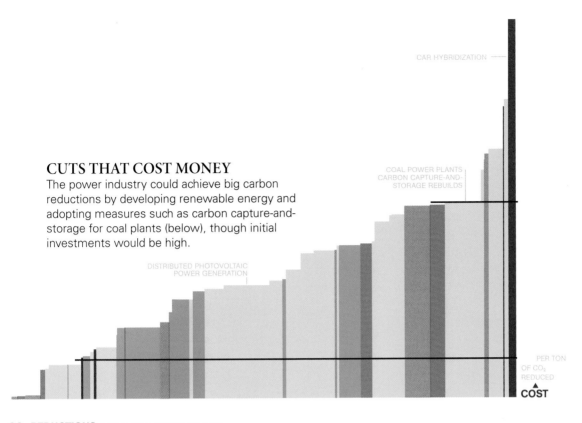

CAR HYBRIDIZATION

COAL POWER PLANTS CARBON CAPTURE-AND-STORAGE REBUILDS

DISTRIBUTED PHOTOVOLTAIC POWER GENERATION

PER TON OF CO_2 REDUCED

COST

CO_2 REDUCTIONS ▶ (IN BILLIONS OF TONS PER YEAR)

A worker in Washington, D.C., installs a triple-glazed window in a structure designed to meet strict "green building" standards. Advanced lighting, heating, cooling, and water systems—as well as a green roof—contribute to a small carbon footprint. This can reduce energy costs by up to 75 percent. But many firms hesitate to invest in efficiency if up-front costs seem too high or payback times too long.

(Continued from page 50) "If you can get enough people to do things in enough communities, you can have a huge impact," said David Gershon, author of *Low Carbon Diet: A 30-Day Program to Lose 5,000 Pounds.* "When people are successful, they say, 'Wow, I want to go further. I'm going to push for better public transportation, bike lanes, whatever.' Somebody called this the mice-on-the-ice strategy. You don't have to get any one element to work, but if you come at it from enough different directions, eventually the ice cracks."

Will it make any difference? That's what we really wanted to know. Our low carbon diet had shown us that, with little or no hardship and no major cash outlays, we could cut day-to-day emissions of CO_2 in half—mainly by wasting less energy at home and on the highway. Similar efforts in office buildings, shopping malls, and factories throughout the nation, combined with incentives and efficiency standards, could halt further increases in U.S. emissions.

That won't be enough by itself, though. The world will still suffer severe disruptions unless humanity reduces emissions sharply—and they've risen 30 percent since 1990. As much as 80 percent of new energy demand in the next decade is projected to come from China, India, and other developing nations. China is building the equivalent of two mid-size coal-fired power plants a week, and by 2007 its CO_2 output surpassed that of the U.S. Putting the brakes on global emissions will be more difficult than curbing CO_2 in the United States, because the economies of developing nations are growing faster. But it begins the same way: By focusing on better insulation in houses, more efficient lights in offices, better gas mileage in cars, and smarter processes in industry. The potential exists, as McKinsey

I hadn't expected that a modern aircraft would emit **almost half as much CO_2 per person** as we would have produced if we'd driven to Oregon and back in our car.

reported last year, to cut the growth of global emissions in half.

Yet efficiency, in the end, can only take us so far. To get the deeper reductions we need, as Tim Flannery advised—80 percent by 2050 (or even 100 percent, as he now advocates)—we must replace fossil fuels faster with renewable energy from wind farms, solar plants, geothermal facilities, and biofuels. We must slow deforestation, which is an additional source of greenhouse gases. And we must develop technologies to capture and bury carbon dioxide from existing power plants. Efficiency can buy us time—perhaps as much as two decades—to figure out how to remove carbon from the world's diet.

The rest of the world isn't waiting for the United States to show the way. Sweden has pioneered carbon-neutral houses, Germany affordable solar power, Japan fuel-efficient cars, the Netherlands prosperous cities filled with bicycles. Do Americans have the will to match such efforts?

Maybe so, said R. James Woolsey, former director of the CIA, who sees a powerful, if unlikely, new alliance forming behind energy efficiency. "Some people are in favor of it because it's a way to make money, some because they're worried about terrorism or global warming, some because they think it's their religious duty," he said. "But it's all coming together, and politicians are starting to notice. I call it a growing coalition between the tree huggers, the do-gooders, the sodbusters, the cheap hawks, the evangelicals, the utility shareholders, the mom-and-pop drivers, and Willie Nelson."

This movement starts at home with the changing of a lightbulb, the opening of a window, a walk to the bus, or a bike ride to the post office. PJ and I did it for only a month, but I can see the low carbon diet becoming a habit.

"What do we have to lose?" PJ said.

Discussion Questions

- How much CO_2 does the average American household emit, and how does that compare to the rest of the world?

- What are some ways to reduce household energy use?

- What is "vampire power," and how much energy does it commonly use?

- What are the three major sources of carbon emissions, and how do they compare to one another?

- Discuss the trend amongst developing countries, such as China and India, in contributing to global carbon emissions.

Challenges and Solutions

- Use the EPA Household Emissions Calculator (http://www.epa.gov/ climatechange/emissions/ind_calculator. html) to estimate the carbon emissions generated in your home. Propose four or five ways you could reduce these emissions and discuss the plausibility of each.

Social Implications

- Identify the social implications of sharply reducing carbon emissions. Would such changes be socially acceptable? Do the efforts of individuals really make a difference?

VIKING WEATHER

Greenland plays a pivotal role in the future of global climate change. Its landmass is largely covered in a thick ice sheet, and it is melting rapidly. The melting of Greenland will have major impacts on coastal communities around the globe. At the same time, Greenlanders who have traditionally had very limited access to resources offer a unique perspective on the warming of the planet.

As you read "Viking Weather," consider the following questions:

- How much ice covers Greenland?
- How much water does this ice sheet hold?
- To what extent could the melting of Greenland cause sea levels to rise?
- What effect would the melting of the ice sheet have on Greenland's access to oil and mineral reserves?
- Global climate change will affect Greenland in many ways; in what ways will the melting of Greenland's ice influence the rest of the world?

A September storm darkens Tasermiut fjord.

VIKING
WEATHER

By Tim Folger

Photographs by Peter Essick

On a dog day afternoon in Qaqortoq, a town of 3,500 in southern Greenland, the reservoir becomes a swimming hole. The snowmelt that fills it can warm to as much as 50°F.

AS GREENLAND RETURNS TO THE WARM
CLIMATE THAT ALLOWED VIKINGS TO COLONIZE IT
IN THE MIDDLE AGES,

ITS ISOLATED AND DEPENDENT PEOPLE DREAM OF GREENER FIELDS AND PASTURES–
AND ALSO OF OIL FROM ICE-FREE WATERS.

A little north and west of Greenland's stormy southern tip, on a steep hillside above an iceberg-clotted fjord first explored by Erik the Red more than a thousand years ago, sprout some horticultural anomalies: a trim lawn of Kentucky bluegrass, some rhubarb, and a few spruce, poplar, fir, and willow trees. They're in the town of Qaqortoq, 60° 43' north latitude, in Kenneth Høegh's backyard, about 400 miles south of the Arctic Circle.

"We had frost last night," Høegh says as we walk around his yard on a warm July morning, examining his plants while mosquitoes examine us. Qaqortoq's harbor glitters sapphire blue below us in the bright sun. A small iceberg—about the size of a city bus—has drifted within a few feet of the town's dock. Brightly painted clapboard homes, built with wood imported from Europe, freckle the nearly bare granite hills that rise like an amphitheater over the harbor.

Høegh, a powerfully built man with reddish blond hair and a trim beard—he could easily be cast as a Viking—is an agronomist and former chief adviser to Greenland's agriculture ministry. His family has lived in Qaqortoq for more than 200 years. Pausing near the edge of

Yet in Greenland itself, apprehension about climate change is often overshadowed by great expectations.

the yard, Høegh kneels and peers under a white plastic sheet that protects some turnips he planted last month.

"Wooo! This is quite incredible!" he says with a broad smile. The turnips' leaves look healthy and green. "I haven't looked at them for three or four weeks; I didn't water the garden at all this year. Just rainfall and melting snow. This is amazing. We can harvest them right now, no problem."

It's a small thing, the early ripening of turnips on a summer morning—but in a country where some 80 percent of the land lies buried beneath an ice sheet up to two miles thick and where some people have never touched a tree, it stands for a large thing. Greenland is warming twice as fast as most of the world. Satellite measurements show that its vast ice sheet, which holds nearly 7 percent of the world's fresh water, is shrinking by about 50 cubic miles each year. The melting ice accelerates the warming—newly exposed ocean and land absorb sunlight that the ice used to reflect into space. If all of Greenland's ice melts in

Adapted from "Viking Weather" by Tim Folger: National Geographic Magazine, June 2010.

Erik the Red killed a man in Iceland over a trifle and worshipped Norse gods until the end, but at Qassiarsuk (top), site of his Greenland farm, there is a replica of the tiny wood church he built for his wife, who converted to Christianity. A wall kept out the livestock. A cold millennium later in the same area, a soccer fan in Qaqortoq cheers his nephew's team (bottom).

the centuries ahead, sea level will rise by 24 feet, inundating coastlines around the planet.

Yet in Greenland itself, apprehension about climate change is often overshadowed by great expectations. For now this self-governing dependency of Denmark still leans heavily on its former colonial ruler. Denmark pumps $620 million into Greenland's anemic economy every year—more than $11,000 for each Greenlander. But the Arctic meltdown has already started to open up access to oil, gas, and mineral resources that could give Greenland the financial and political independence its people crave. Greenland's coastal waters are estimated to hold half as much oil as the North Sea's fields. Warmer temperatures would also mean a longer growing season for Greenland's 50 or so farms and perhaps reduce the country's utter reliance on imported food. At times these days it feels as if the whole country is holding its breath—waiting to see whether the "greening of Greenland," so regularly announced in the international press, is actually going to happen.

Greenland's first experience of hype happened a millennium ago when Erik the Red arrived from Iceland with a small party of Norsemen, aka Vikings. Erik was on the lam (from the Old Norse word *lemja*) for killing a man who had refused to return some borrowed bedsteads. In 982 he landed along a fjord near Qaqortoq, and then, despite the bedsteads incident, he returned to Iceland to spread word about the country he had found, which, according to the *Saga of Erik the Red,* "he called Greenland, as he said people would be attracted there if it had a favorable name."

Erik's bald-faced marketing worked. Some 4,000 Norse eventually settled in Greenland. The Vikings, notwithstanding their reputation for ferocity, were essentially farmers who did

It feels as if Greenland is holding its breath— waiting to see if the "greening" will actually happen.

a bit of pillaging, plundering, and New World discovering on the side. Along the sheltered fjords of southern and western Greenland, they raised sheep and some cattle, which is what farmers in Greenland do today along the very same fjords. They built churches and hundreds of farms; they traded sealskins and walrus ivory for timber and iron from Europe. Erik's son Leif set out from a farm about 35 miles northeast of Qaqortoq and discovered North America sometime around 1000. In Greenland the Norse settlements held on for more than four centuries. Then, abruptly, they vanished.

The demise of those tough, seafaring farmers offers an unsettling example of the threats climate change poses to even the most resourceful cultures. The Vikings settled Greenland during a period of exceptional warmth, the same warm period that saw expanded agriculture and the construction of great cathedrals in Europe. By 1300, though, Greenland became much colder, and living there became ever more challenging. The Inuit, who had arrived from northern Canada in the meantime, pushing south along the west coast of Greenland as the Vikings pushed north, fared much better. (Modern Greenlanders are mostly descended from them and from Danish missionaries and colonists who arrived in the 18th century.) The Inuit brought with them dogsleds, kayaks, and other essential tools for hunting and fishing in the Arctic. Some researchers have argued that the Norse settlers failed because they remained fatally attached to their old Scandinavian ways, relying heavily on imported farm animals instead of exploiting local resources.

But more recent archaeological evidence suggests the Norse too were well adapted to their new home. Thomas McGovern, an anthropologist at Hunter College in Manhattan, says the Norse organized annual communal hunts for harbor seals, especially once the climate cooled and domestic (Continued on page 64)

Sporting a Thor's hammer amulet, Sten Pedersen picks cabbage, a new crop for Greenland. He'll deliver it to a restaurant in nearby Nuuk, the capital. The edge of the ice sheet lies just 12 miles away.

(*Continued from page 61*) livestock began to die. Unfortunately, harbor seals also succumbed. "Adult harbor seals can survive cold summers, but their pups can't," says McGovern. The Norse may have been forced to extend their hunts farther offshore in search of other seal species, in waters that were becoming more stormy.

"We now think the Norse had a very refined social system that required lots of community labor, but there was a major vulnerability—they had to have most of their adults out there trying to get the seals," says McGovern. "A trigger for the end of the Norse in Greenland could have been catastrophic loss of life from one bad storm." The Inuit would have been less vulnerable because they tended to hunt in small groups. "It's a much more complicated story than we thought," McGovern says. "The old story was just, the silly Vikings come north, screw up, and die. But the new story actually is a bit scarier, because they look pretty well adapted, well organized, doing a lot of things right—and they die anyway."

The last historically documented event of Norse life in Greenland was not a perfect storm, though, nor a famine nor an exodus to Europe. It was a wedding held at a church near the head of Hvalsey fjord, about ten miles northeast of Qaqortoq. Much of the church still stands on a grassy slope beneath a towering granite peak.

On a cool morning last summer a strand of fog lingered high up on the peak's eastern face like a gossamer pennant. Wild thyme with delicate, purple-red flowers spread low across the ground in front of the 800-year-old church, now roofed only by sky. All four of the three-foot-thick, stone-slab walls remain intact—the eastern wall is about 18 feet tall. They were evidently built by people who intended to stay here a while. Within the walls, grass and sheep droppings cover the uneven ground where, on September 14, 1408, Thorstein Olafsson married Sigrid Bjørnsdottir. A letter sent from Greenland to Iceland in 1424 mentions the

wedding, perhaps as part of an inheritance dispute, but provides no news of strife, disease, or any inkling of impending disaster. Nothing more was ever heard from the Norse settlements.

Greenlanders today, all 56,000 of them, still live on the rocky fringes between ice and sea, most in a handful of towns along the west coast. Glaciers and a coastline deeply indented by fjords make it impossible to build roads between the towns; everyone travels by boat, helicopter, plane, or, in the winter, dogsled. More than a quarter of all Greenlanders, some 15,500, live in Nuuk, Greenland's capital, about 300 miles north of Qaqortoq as the narwhal swims.

Take one part quaint Greenlandic town, complete with fjord and exhilarating mountainous backdrop, mix with maybe four parts grim Soviet-bloc-style apartments, add two traffic lights, daily traffic jams, and a nine-hole golf course, and you've got Nuuk. The sprawling, run-down apartment blocks are a legacy of a forced modernization program from the 1950s and 1960s, when the Danish government moved people from small traditional communities into a few large towns. The intent was to improve access to schools and health care, reduce costs, and provide employees for processing plants in the cod-fishing industry, which boomed in the early 1960s but has since collapsed. Whatever benefits the policy brought, it bred a host of social problems—alcoholism, fractured families, suicide—that still plague Greenland.

But this morning, on the first day of summer 2009, the mood in Nuuk is jubilant: Greenland is celebrating the start of a new era. In November 2008 its citizens voted overwhelmingly for increased independence from Denmark, which has ruled Greenland in some form since 1721. The change is to become official this morning in a ceremony at Nuuk's harbor, the heart of the old colonial town. Queen Margrethe II of Denmark will formally acknowledge the new relationship between her country and Kalaallit Nunaat, as the locals call their homeland.

Per Rosing, a slender 58-year-old Inuit man with a gentle manner and a graying black ponytail, conducts the Greenland National Choir. "I'm just happy, totally happy," he says, putting a hand over his heart as we walk with a large crowd toward the harbor, down streets still wet from last night's freezing rain and snow. People are streaming out of Block P, Nuuk's biggest apartment building, which alone houses about one percent of Greenland's population. Its windowless, concrete end has become a frame for a defiantly optimistic work of art: a four-story-tall, white-and-red Greenlandic flag. A local artist sewed the flag with the help of schoolchildren from hundreds of articles of clothing.

By 7:30 people are packed shoulder to shoulder on the dock. Others perch on the roofs of old wooden homes around the harbor; a few watch from kayaks, paddling just enough to stay put in calm,

metallic-looking water. The ceremony begins with the choir singing Greenland's national anthem, "Nunarput Utoqqarsuanngoravit—You, Our Ancient Land." Rosing turns to the crowd and gestures for everyone to join in. As of today, Kalaallisut, an Inuit dialect, is the official Greenlandic language, supplanting Danish.

Then, shortly after eight o'clock, the Danish queen, wearing the traditional Inuit garb of a married woman—red, thigh-high, sealskin boots, or kamiks, a beaded shawl, and seal-fur shorts—presents the new self-government charter to Josef Tuusi Motzfeldt, the speaker of Greenland's Parliament. The crowd cheers, and a cannon fires on a hill above the harbor, sending a pressure wave through us like a shared infusion of adrenaline.

Under the new charter, Denmark still manages Greenland's foreign policy; the annual subsidy continues as well. But Greenland now exerts greater control over its own domestic affairs—and in particular, over its vast mineral resources. Without them, there's no chance that Greenland could ever become economically independent. Right now fishing accounts for more than 80 percent of Greenland's export income; shrimp and halibut are the mainstays. While halibut stocks are holding steady, shrimp populations have dropped. Royal Greenland, the state-owned fishing company, is bleeding money.

The reasons for the decline of the shrimp—known here as "pink gold"—are unclear. Søren Rysgaard, director of the Greenland Climate Research Center in Nuuk, says that Greenland's climate, besides getting warmer, is becoming more unpredictable. Rising sea temperatures may have disrupted the timing between the hatching of shrimp larvae and the blooms of phytoplankton the larvae feed on; no one really knows. Fishermen hope cod will return as waters warm. But after a small uptick a few years ago, cod numbers have fallen again. *(Continued on page 68)*

Sheep are rounded up near Qassiarsuk, where Erik the Red raised cattle. Greenland spends nearly two million dollars a year subsidizing its 50 sheep farms, which import much of their fodder.

Haymaking time in Greenland evokes the sunny side of global warming, which just might allow Aviaja Lennert and her family to grow enough grass for their 700 sheep.

(Continued from page 65) "The traditional way of life in Greenland was based on stability," says Rysgaard. Apart from southern Greenland, which has always been swept by Atlantic storms, the climate, although formidably cold, seldom surprised. The huge ice sheet, with its attendant mass of cold, dense air, enforced stability over most of the country. "In the winter you could hunt or fish with your sled dogs on the sea ice. In the summer you could hunt from a kayak. What's happening now is that the instability typical of southern Greenland is moving north."

Johannes Mathæussen, a 47-year-old Inuit halibut fisherman, has seen those changes firsthand. Mathæussen lives in Ilulissat (Greenlandic for "icebergs"), a town of 4,500 people and almost that many sled dogs located 185 miles north of the Arctic Circle. On an overcast day in late June we set out from Ilulissat's harbor, motoring past a big shrimp trawler in Mathæussen's 15-foot-long open boat, a typical craft for halibut fishermen here. Summer fishing is still good for them, but winter is becoming a problem.

"Twenty years ago, in the winter, you could drive a car over the ice to Disko Island," Mathæussen says, pointing to a large island about 30 miles off the coast. "For 10 of the last 12 years, the bay has not frozen over in the winter." When the bay used to freeze, Mathæussen and other fishermen would rig their dogsleds and go ice fishing ten miles up the fjord. "I would spend a day and a night and bring back 200 or 500 pounds of halibut on my sled. Now winter fishing in the fjord is dangerous with a heavy load; the ice is too thin."

Mathæussen steers his boat through a broken canyon of ice that is drifting imperceptibly out to sea. The largest bergs rise 200 feet above us with keels scraping the bottom 600 feet down. Each one has its own topography of hills, cliffs, caves, and arroyos of smooth white flanks polished by meltwater streams. All this ice comes from Jakobshavn Isbræ, aka Sermeq Kujalleq, the "southern glacier," which drains 7 percent of Greenland's ice sheet and launches more icebergs than any other Northern Hemisphere glacier. (The iceberg that sank the *Titanic* probably calved here.) In the past decade Sermeq Kujalleq has retreated almost ten miles up the fjord. It is Greenland's biggest tourist draw—19,375 people came to see global warming in action here in 2008. Tourism remains a distant second to fishing, though; the season is short, accommodations are limited, and travel is expensive.

The foundation of Greenland's future economy lies out beyond Disko Island, just over the horizon from Mathæussen's spectacular fishing ground: That's where the oil is. The sea off the central west coast now typically remains ice free for nearly half the year, a month longer than 25 years ago. With the greater ease of working in Greenland's waters, ExxonMobil, Chevron, and other oil companies have acquired exploration licenses. Cairn Energy, a Scottish company, plans to drill its first exploration wells this year.

"We've issued 13 licenses covering 130,000 square kilometers off the west coast, roughly three times the size of mainland Denmark," says Jørn Skov Nielsen, director of Greenland's Bureau of Minerals and Petroleum. We're at a bustling trade convention in a conference center in Nuuk on a rainy Saturday afternoon. The smell of oil wafts from a rock sample—a chunk of basalt the size and shape of half a bowling ball—that is displayed on a nearby table. "Production could be possible in ten years if we're lucky," Nielsen says. "We have some very impressive estimates for northwest and northeast Greenland—50 billion barrels of oil and gas." With oil prices now topping

Greenland's future may lie out **beyond its spectacular fishing grounds: That's where the oil is.**

$80 a barrel, those reserves would be worth more than four trillion dollars, a windfall that could fund the country's independence.

To some Greenlanders it would be a Faustian bargain. Sofie Petersen, the Lutheran bishop, has an office overlooking the harbor in one of Nuuk's few surviving old wooden homes. Just up the hill stands a statue of Hans Egede, a quixotic Lutheran missionary who came here in 1721 looking for survivors of the lost Norse settlements. He found no Norsemen but founded Nuuk, or Godthåb, as the Danes called it, and set in motion the Danish colonization of Greenland and its conversion to Christianity. Like nearly all Greenlanders, Petersen has a Danish surname, but she is Inuit.

"I think oil will damage our way of living," she says. "Of course everyone needs money, but should we sell our souls? What will happen if we are millionaires, every one of us, and we can't deliver Greenland as we know it to our grandchildren? I would rather have little money and give the land to our grandchildren instead."

"It's a big dilemma to deal with the oil issue, since the Arctic people are the ones most exposed to climate change," says Kuupik Kleist, Greenland's popular new prime minister. Sometimes called Greenland's Leonard Cohen—he has recorded a few CDs—Kleist is a broadly built, owlish man of 52 with a husky, sonorous voice. The irony in his country becoming a major producer of the very stuff that is helping to melt its ice sheet is not lost on him.

"We need a stronger economy," Kleist says, "and we have to utilize the opportunities that oil could bring to us. Environmentalists around the world advise us not to exploit the oil reserves. But we are not in the situation where we can replace the declining income from our fisheries, and we don't have any other resources for the time being that hold as much potential as oil."

Actually there is one other resource with enormous potential, but it is equally fraught. Greenland Minerals and Energy Ltd., an Australian company, has discovered what may be the world's largest deposit of rare earth metals on a plateau above the town of Narsaq in southern Greenland. The rare earths are crucial in a wide variety of green technologies—hybrid-car batteries, wind turbines, and compact fluorescent lightbulbs—and China now controls more than 95 percent of the world's supply.

The development of the deposit at Narsaq would fundamentally shift global markets and transform Greenland's economy. John Mair, general manager of Greenland Minerals and Energy, says that Narsaq's reserves could sustain a large-scale mining operation for well over 50 years, employing hundreds in a town that has been devastated by the collapse of cod fishing. His company has dozens of employees prospecting the site right now. But there is a major obstacle to developing it: The ore is also laced with uranium, and Greenland's government has a complete ban on uranium mining. "We haven't changed those regulations and are not planning to," Kleist says. There is no easy path, it seems, to a greener Greenland, in any sense of the word.

Greenlanders jokingly call the area around Narsaq and Qaqortoq, Sineriak Banaaneqarfik, the Banana Coast. Today the grandchildren of Inuit hunters till fields there, along fjords where Vikings once farmed. If Greenland is greening anywhere, it is here. But as soon as I arrive, the agronomist Kenneth Høegh cautions me to forget what I've read about Greenland's sudden cornucopia. "Arctic Harvest," read one headline; "In Greenland, Potatoes Thrive," read another. Potatoes do grow in Greenland these days. But not so very many just yet.

I ask the farmer if global warming will make life easier. "Last year we almost had a catastrophe," he says.

On a gorgeous July morning Høegh and I are cruising at about 25 knots up the fjord settled by Erik the Red a millennium ago. Our destination is Ipiutaq, population three. Kalista Poulsen is waiting for us on a rocky outcrop below his farm on the northern shore of the fjord. Even in faded gray overalls, Poulsen looks more like a scholar than a farmer: He's slender, wears glasses, and speaks English with what sounds, strangely enough, like a French accent. His great-great-grandfather was an *angakkoq*—a shaman—one of the last in Greenland, who had killed men in feuds before converting to Christianity after having a vision of Jesus.

We walk through Poulsen's lush fields of timothy and ryegrass. Compared with the fjord's sheer gray walls, the fodder crops look almost fluorescent. In September Poulsen will acquire his first sheep, which is what nearly all of Greenland's farmers raise, mostly for meat. He bought the farm in 2005, as the outside world was first hearing talk of a gentler, warmer Greenland.

From where Poulsen stands, the promise seems remote. "This is my war zone," he says, as we trudge across muddy, boulder-strewn ground that he's clearing for cultivation with a backhoe and a tractor with big tillers he had delivered on old military landing craft. When I ask Poulsen if he thinks global warming will make life easier for him or his child, his expression becomes almost pained. He looks at me appraisingly as he lights a cigarette, which momentarily disperses a cloud of mosquitoes.

"Last year we almost had a catastrophe," he says. "It was so dry the harvest was only half of normal. I don't think we can count on normal weather. If it's getting warmer, we'll have to water more, invest in a watering system. In the winter we don't have normal snow; it rains, and then it freezes. That's not good for the grass. It's just exposed in the cold."

Over lunch in Poulsen's white wood-frame home, the mystery of his French accent is solved: Agathe Devisme, *(Continued on page 74)*

An Inuit boy from a foster home in Nuuk learns hunting from a mentor; here they've bagged a caribou (top). Most Greenland-ers hunt, and fishing is by far the dominant industry. Workers at the city's Royal Greenland plant package whole, frozen cod for export. High labor costs make it cheaper to ship the fish to China or Poland for processing (bottom).

On a cool day in August, descendants of Inuit hunters harvest potatoes along a fjord the Vikings settled. Despite a modest rise in farm output, Greenland still imports nearly all its produce.

Rain blurs the view of icebergs in Narsaq, where a mysterious decline in shrimp has shuttered a processing plant and left dozens of residents pondering an uncertain future.

(Continued from page 70) his companion, is French. Savoring the fusion meal she has prepared—shrimp and catfish au gratin, *mattak,* or raw whale skin, and apple cake flavored with wild angelica—I think back to the more rustic dinner I'd enjoyed a few nights earlier in Qaqortoq, at an annual gala attended by nearly every farming family on the Banana Coast. After dinner a white-haired Inuit man had begun playing an accordion, and everyone in the hall, some 450 people, had linked arms, swaying side to side as they sang a traditional Greenlandic paean:

Summer, summer, how wonderful
How incredibly good.
The frost is gone,
The frost is gone…

Leaving the Poulsens, Høegh and I run back down the fjord with the *føn*—the wind off the ice sheet—at our stern. Høegh would be happy, he had said earlier, if Greenland's farms were to get to the point where they grow most of their own winter fodder for their sheep and cattle; many farms, far from feeding their countrymen, now import more than half their fodder from Europe. In Høegh's house that evening we stand looking out the window at his garden. The føn has become fierce. Horizontal sheets of rain flatten his rhubarb and his turnips; his trees bend like supplicants before implacable old gods. "Damn!" Høegh says quietly. "The weather's tough here. It will always be tough."

Discussion Questions

- Discuss the link between climate change and shrimp population decline.

- What are the impacts of declining winter ice on the population of Greenland?

- How does climate change relate to the prosperity of Greenland?

- Discuss the impacts of climate change on agriculture and food production in Greenland.

- Discuss the full scope of the global changes that would come as a result of the "greening of Greenland."

Challenges and Solutions

Identify the positive and negative effects of climate change in Greenland, and indicate how they might influence life for Greenlanders.

Social Implications

Identify the social implications of climate change in Greenland and how various stakeholders or interest groups might be affected (e.g. farmers, fishermen, Greenlanders in general). Choose one of these groups and explore their perspective. Assume that this group is taking their issue to the annual global climate change summit, and they wish to issue a press release about their concerns. Write that press release and either a) submit it as a paper, b) give a group presentation to the course, or c) post it to the course blog as directed by your instructor.

THE COMING STORM

It is expected that there will be 250 million climate refugees by the middle of the century. Bangladesh is poised to contribute greatly to that number, as its already dense population continues to grow, and its low-lying landmass becomes inundated by rising sea levels driven by global climate change.

As you read "The Coming Storm," consider the following questions:

- Why is the adaptability of the people of Bangladesh seen as a model for the developed world as it begins to feel the effects of climate change?
- What two factors are predicted to have changed dramatically for Bangladesh by 2050?
- How can Bangladesh diminish the size of its population, and thus reduce the number of climate refugees?
- Have developed nations committed to allocating funds to alleviate the affects of climate change on the poor nations that will be most affected? To what extent would this affect Bangladesh?
- In what ways can Bangladesh's situation be applied as a model for the developed world as it adapts to the affects of climate change?

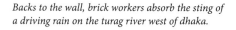

*Backs to the wall, brick workers absorb the sting of
a driving rain on the turag river west of dhaka.*

THE
COMING
STORM

By Don Belt

Photographs By Jonas Bendiksen

OVERFLOWING WITH PEOPLE
*Taxi boats called kheya nouka cross the Buriganga River to
Sadar Ghat, Dhaka's main boat terminal, providing transport
in one of the world's most densely populated cities. Low-lying
Dhaka is among those most at risk from rising seas.*

THE PEOPLE OF BANGLADESH HAVE MUCH TO
TEACH US ABOUT

HOW A CROWDED PLANET CAN BEST ADAPT TO RISING SEA LEVELS.

FOR THEM, THAT FUTURE IS NOW.

We may be seven billion specks on the surface of Earth, but when you're in Bangladesh, it sometimes feels as if half the human race were crammed into a space the size of Louisiana. Dhaka, its capital, is so crowded that every park and footpath has been colonized by the homeless. To stroll here in the mists of early morning is to navigate an obstacle course of makeshift beds and sleeping children. Later the city's steamy roads and alleyways clog with the chaos of some 15 million people, most of them stuck in traffic. Amid this clatter and hubbub moves a small army of Bengali beggars, vegetable sellers, popcorn vendors, rickshaw drivers, and trinket salesmen, all surging through the city like particles in a flash flood. The countryside beyond is a vast watery floodplain with intermittent stretches of land that are lush, green, flat as a parking lot—and wall-to-wall with human beings. In places you might expect to find solitude, there is none. There are no lonesome highways in Bangladesh.

It is a place where one person, in a nation of 164 million, is mathematically incapable of being truly alone.

We should not be surprised. Bangladesh is, after all, one of the most densely populated nations on Earth. It has more people than geographically massive Russia. It is a place where one person, in a nation of 164 million, is mathematically incapable of being truly alone. That takes some getting used to.

So imagine Bangladesh in the year 2050, when its population will likely have zoomed to 220 million, and a good chunk of its current landmass could be permanently underwater. That scenario is based on two converging projections: population growth that, despite a sharp decline in fertility, will continue to produce millions more Bangladeshis in the coming decades, and a possible multifoot rise in sea level by 2100 as a result of climate change. Such a scenario could mean that 10 to 30 million people along the southern coast would be displaced, forcing Bangladeshis (Continued on page 82)

Adapted from "The Coming Storm" by Don Belt: National Geographic Magazine, May 2011.

SEEKING HIGHER GROUND
Villagers pitch in to relocate buildings on Sirajbag, a silt island in the Jamuna River where flooding is common. Dismantled at noon, this mosque was rebuilt in time for evening prayers.

HOME FOR THE MOMENT
Wading in a foot of water, the Uddin family gathers for a meal. They had recently moved their house to this location to escape flooding on an island near Kurigram. Soon after this photo was taken, the family planned to dismantle the house and move again.

(Continued from page 79) to crowd even closer together or else flee the country as climate refugees—a group predicted to swell to some 250 million worldwide by the middle of the century, many from poor, low-lying countries.

"Globally, we're talking about the largest mass migration in human history," says Maj. Gen. Muniruzzaman, a charismatic retired army officer who presides over the Bangladesh Institute of Peace and Security Studies in Dhaka. "By 2050 millions of displaced people will overwhelm not just our limited land and resources but our government, our institutions, and our borders." Muniruzzaman cites a recent war game run by the National Defense University in Washington, D.C., which forecast the geopolitical chaos that such a mass migration of Bangladeshis might cause in South Asia. In that exercise millions of refugees fled to neighboring India, leading to disease, religious conflict, chronic shortages of food and fresh water, and heightened tensions between the nuclear-armed adversaries India and Pakistan.

Such a catastrophe, even imaginary, fits right in with Bangladesh's crisis-driven story line, which, since the country's independence in 1971, has included war, famine, disease, killer cyclones, massive floods, military coups, political assassinations, and pitiable rates of poverty and deprivation—a list of woes that inspired some to label it an international basket case. Yet if despair is in order, plenty of people in Bangladesh didn't read the script. In fact, many here are pitching another ending altogether, one in which the hardships of their past give rise to a powerful hope.

For all its troubles, Bangladesh is a place where adapting to a changing climate actually seems possible, and where every low-tech adaptation imaginable is now being tried. Supported by governments of the industrialized countries—whose greenhouse emissions are largely responsible for the climate change that is causing seas to rise—and implemented by a long list of international nongovernmental organizations (NGOs), these innovations are gaining credence, thanks to the one commodity that Bangladesh has in profusion: human resilience. Before this century is over, the world, rather than pitying Bangladesh, may wind up learning from her example.

More than a third of the world's people live within 62 miles of a shoreline. Over the coming decades, as sea levels rise, climate change experts predict that many of the world's largest cities, including Miami and New York, will be increasingly vulnerable to coastal flooding. A recent study of 136 port cities found that those with the largest threatened populations will be in developing countries, especially those in Asia. Worldwide, the two cities that will have the greatest proportional increase in people exposed to climate extremes by 2070 are both in Bangladesh: Dhaka and Chittagong, with Khulna close behind. Though some parts of the delta region may keep pace with rising sea levels, thanks to river sediment that builds up coastal land, other areas will likely be submerged.

But Bangladeshis don't have to wait decades for a preview of a future transformed by rising seas. From their vantage point on the Bay of Bengal, they are already facing what it's like to live in an overpopulated and climate-changed world. They've watched sea levels rise, salinity infect their coastal aquifers, river flooding become more destructive, and cyclones batter their coast with increasing intensity—all changes associated with disruptions in the global climate.

On May 25, 2009, the people of Munshiganj, a village of 35,000 on the southwest coast, got a glimpse of what to expect from a multifoot rise in sea level. That morning a cyclone, called Aila, was lurking offshore, and its 70-mile-an-hour winds sent a storm surge racing silently toward shore, where the villagers, unsuspecting, were busy tending their rice fields and repairing their nets.

Shortly after ten o'clock Nasir Uddin, a 40-year-old fisherman, noticed that the tidal river next to the village was rising "much faster than normal" toward high tide. He looked back just in time to see a wall of brown water start pouring over one of the six-foot earthen dikes that protect the village—its last line of defense against the sea.

Within seconds water was surging through his house, sucking away the mud walls and everything else. His three young daughters jumped onto the kitchen table, screaming as cold salt water swirled around their ankles, then up to their knees. "I was sure we were dead," he told me months later, standing in shin-deep mud next to a pond full of stagnant green water the color of antifreeze. "But Allah had other plans."

As if by a miracle, an empty fishing boat swept past, and Uddin grabbed it and hoisted his daughters inside. A few minutes later the boat capsized, but the family managed to hang on as it was tossed by waves. The water finally subsided, leaving hundreds of people dead along the southwest coast and thousands homeless. Uddin and most of his neighbors in Munshiganj decided to hunker down and rebuild, but thousands of others set out to start a new life in inland cities such as Khulna and Dhaka.

Thousands of people arrive in Dhaka each day, fleeing river flooding in the north and cyclones in the south. Many of them end up living in the densely populated slum of Korail. And with hundreds of thousands of such migrants already, Dhaka is in no shape to take in new residents. It's already struggling to provide the most basic services and infrastructure.

Yet precisely because Bangladesh has so many problems, it's long served as a kind

NEPAL

Brahmaputra

Monsoons
Stronger seasonal
rains (June through
September) increase
flooding.

Tista

Kurigram

FLOOD RISK
Depth in feet
DRY 0   1   3   9

AREA OF
DETAIL
EUROPE ASIA
AFRICA
INDIAN
OCEAN

Gaibandha

Jamuna

B A N G L A D E S H

Ganges

Rajshahi

INDIA

Buriganga Turag
River   River

Padma

Dhaka

Meghna

INDIA

CHITTAGONG HILL
TRACTS
Despite a 1997 peace
treaty, tensions remain
between the area's
indigenous peoples
and Bengali settlers.

BORDER FENCE
To block
immigration from
Bangladesh, India is
erecting a six-foot
barrier of barbed
wire and concrete
along the 2,500-
mile border.

Chuknagar   Khulna

Jaliakhali

EXTENT
OF TIDAL
FLOODING

CHITTAGONG HILL TRACTS

Munshiganj

Chittagong

SATKHIRA
DISTRICT

S U N D A R B A N S

Mouths of
the Ganges

CYCLONES
Storm surges and
high tides displace
thousands of people
each year.

POPULATION DENSITY
The country's 164 million
people (more than half
the population of the
U.S.) live in an area
smaller than Utah. Only
the mangrove expanse
of the Sundarbans and
the tribal Chittagong
Hill Tracts are sparsely
populated.

State of Utah at
the same scale

**BANGLADESH:
IN NATURE'S WAY**
On the fertile delta of three major
river systems, Bangladesh is
chronically flooded. In coming
decades, rising sea levels could
permanently uproot millions of
coastal residents.

MYANMA
(BURMA)

WILLIAM E. MCNULTY, NGM STAFF

SOURCES: GOVERNMENT OF BANGLADESH; OAK RIDGE
NATIONAL LABORATORY LANDSCAN 2009 (INSET MAP)

PEOPLE PER SQUARE MILE
1   100   1,000 10,000

CITY BOUND
Under a rainy-season sky, migrants take the train back to Dhaka after visiting their home villages north of the capital. On either side are rice fields, healthy here but tainted by salinity farther south.

of laboratory for innovative solutions in the developing world. It has bounced back from crisis after crisis, proving itself far more resourceful than skeptics might have guessed. Dhaka is home to BRAC, the largest non-profit in the developing world, held up as a model for how to provide basic health care and other services with an army of field-workers. Bangladesh also produced the global micro-finance movement started by Nobel Peace laureate Muhammad Yunus and his Grameen Bank.

And believe it or not, it's a population success story as well. To whittle its high birthrate, Bangladesh developed a grassroots family-planning program in the 1970s that has lowered its fertility rate from 6.6 children per woman in 1977 to about 2.4 today—a historic record for a country with so much poverty and illiteracy. Fertility decline has generally been associated with economic improvement, which prompts parents to limit family size so they can provide education and other opportunities to their children. But Bangladesh has been able to reduce fertility despite its lack of economic development.

"It was very hard in the beginning," says Begum Rokeya, 42, a government health worker in the Satkhira District who's made thousands of home visits to persuade new-lywed couples to use contraception and plan their family's size. "This is a very conservative country, and men put pressure on women to have lots of children. But they began to see that if they immunized their kids, they wouldn't need to have a bunch of babies just so a few would survive. They like the idea of fewer mouths to feed."

Working in partnership with dozens of NGOs, Bangladesh has *(Continued on page 88)*

AT A BREAKING POINT
Dhaka slums such as Korail (foreground) are bursting with environmental refugees, putting more pressure on a city laid low by aging infrastructure, intense poverty, and frequent flooding.

Urban Challenge
Sanitation systems are faltering as Bangladeshis crowd into cities.

NGM ART
SOURCE: WORLD HEALTH ORGANIZATION

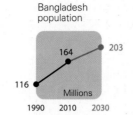

Bangladesh population

164
203
116
Millions
1990 2010 2030

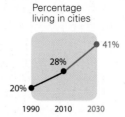

Percentage living in cities

41%
28%
20%
1990 2010 2030

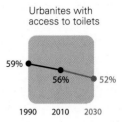

Urbanites with access to toilets

59%
56%
52%
1990 2010 2030

(Continued from page 85) made huge strides in educating women and providing them with economic opportunities; female work-participation rates have doubled since 1995. Its economy is growing, helped by its garment-export industry. And Bangladesh has managed to meet an important UN Millennium Development Goal: Infant mortality dropped dramatically between 1990 and 2008, from 100 deaths per 1,000 births to 43—one of the highest improvement rates among low-income countries.

In Dhaka such successes are dwarfed by the overwhelming poverty and the constant influx of villagers, prompting organizations, including BRAC, to get involved in helping village people figure out how to survive in a deteriorating environment. "Our goal is to prevent people from coming to Dhaka in the first place, by helping them adapt and find new ways of making a go of it in their villages," says Babar Kabir, head of BRAC's climate change and disaster management programs. "Big storms like Aila uproot them from the lives they know."

Ibrahim Khalilullah has lost track of how many times he's moved. "Thirty? Forty?" he asks. "Does it matter?" Actually those figures might be a bit low, as he estimates he's moved about once a year his whole life, and he's now over 60. Somehow, between all that moving, he and his wife raised seven children who "never missed a meal," he says proudly. He's a warm, good-natured man, with gray hair cut short and a longish gray beard, and everything he says has a note of joy in it.

Khalilullah is a char dweller, one of the hundreds of thousands of people who inhabit the constantly changing islands, or chars, on the floodplains of Bangladesh's three major rivers—the Padma, Jamuna, and Meghna. These islands, many covering less than a square mile, appear and vanish constantly, rising and falling with the tide, the season, the phase of the moon, the rainfall, and the flow of rivers upstream. Char dwellers will set out by boat to visit friends on another char, only to find that it's completely disappeared. Later they will hear through the grapevine that their friends moved to a new char that had popped up a few miles downstream, built their house in a day, and planted a garden by nightfall. Making a life on the chars—growing crops, building a home, raising a family—is like winning an Olympic medal in adaptation. Char dwellers may be the most resilient people on Earth.

There are tricks to living on a char, Khalilullah says. He builds his house in sections that can be dismantled, moved, and reassembled in a matter of a few hours. He always builds on a raised platform of earth at least six feet high. He uses sheets of corrugated metal for the outside walls and panels of thatch for the roof. He keeps the family suitcases stacked neatly next to the bed in case they're needed on short notice. And he has documents, passed down from his father, that establish his right to settle on new islands when they emerge—part of an intricate system of laws and customs that would prevent a million migrants from the south, say, from ever squatting on the chars. His real secret, he says, is not to think too much. "We're all under pressure, but there's really no point to worry. This is our only option, to move from place to place to place. We farm this land for as long as we can, and then the river washes it away. No matter how much we worry, the ending is always the same."

Even in the best of times, it's a precarious way of life. And these are not the best of times. In Bangladesh climate change threatens not just the coast but also inland communities like Khalilullah's. It could disrupt natural cycles of precipitation, including monsoon rains and the Tibetan Plateau snowfall, both of which feed the major rivers that eventually braid their way through the delta.

But precisely because the country's geography is prone to floods and cyclones, Bangladeshis have gotten a head start on preparing for a climate-changed future. For decades they have been developing more salt-resistant strains of rice and building dikes to keep low-lying farms from being flooded with seawater. As a result, the country has actually doubled its production of rice since the early 1970s. Similarly its frequent cyclones have prompted it to build cyclone shelters and develop early-warning systems for natural disasters. More recently various NGOs have set up floating schools, hospitals, and libraries that keep right on functioning through monsoon season.

"Let me tell you about Bangladeshis," says Zakir Kibria, 37, a political scientist who serves as a policy analyst at Uttaran, an NGO devoted to environmental justice and poverty eradication. "We may be poor and appear disorganized, but we are not victims. And when things get tough, people here do what they've always done—they find a way to adapt and survive. We're masters of 'climate resilience.'"

Muhammad Hayat Ali is a 40-year-old farmer, straight as bamboo, who lives east of Satkhira, about 30 miles upstream of the coast but still within range of tidal surges and the salinity of a slowly rising sea. "In previous times this land was juicy, all rice fields," Ali says, his arm sweeping the landscape. "But now the weather has changed—summer is longer and hotter than it used to be, and the rains aren't coming when they should. The rivers are saltier than before, and any water we get from the ground is too salty to grow rice. So now I'm raising shrimps in these ponds and growing my vegetables on the embankments around them." A decade ago such a pond would have been a novelty; now everyone, it seems, is raising shrimps or crabs and selling them to wholesalers for shipment to Dhaka or abroad.

Sometimes, though, adaptations backfire. Throughout southern Bangladesh, villages and fields are shielded from rivers by a network of dikes built by the government with help from Dutch engineers in the 1960s. During floods the rivers sometimes overflow the dikes and fill the fields like soup bowls. When the flood recedes, the water is trapped. The fields become waterlogged, unusable for years at a time.

Decades ago things got so bad in Satkhira—so many fields were waterlogged, so many farmers out of work—that members of the local community used picks and shovels to illegally cut a 20-yard gap in an embankment, draining a huge field that had been waterlogged for nearly three years. In doing so, they were emulating Bengali farmers of earlier times, who periodically broke their embankments and allowed river water to enter their fields, rising and falling with the tides, until the deposited sediment raised the level of the land. But this time the villagers were charged with breaking the law.

Then a funny thing happened. The field, which had been left open, acquired tons of sediment from the river and grew higher by five or six feet. The river channel deepened, and fishermen began to catch *(Continued on page 96)*

(Continued on page 96)

> We may be poor and appear disorganized, but we are not victims. And when things get tough, people here do what they've always done—they find a way to adapt and survive.

HIGH AND DRY
When the river floods, the children of Jabed Ali know what to do: Climb the bamboo macha in the front yard and hold on tight. Midstream-island dwellers are used to such calamities, which are on the increase.

KEEPING A COUNTRY AFLOAT
An army of health workers trained by BRAC, a homegrown nongovernmental organization (NGO), have helped reduce both infant mortality and the birthrate (top left). In the briny south, farmers have converted waterlogged rice fields into ponds for salt-tolerant shrimps and crabs. Enterprising island inhabitants in the Gaibandha District use hyacinth plants to create floating gardens, where they will plant squash, okra, and other food crops (top right). Docking six days a week, a solar-powered school boat (bottom right) helps educate kids whose homes are periodically flooded.

(Continued from page 89) fish again. Finally a government study group came to survey the situation and wound up recommending that other fields be managed the same way. The villagers were vindicated, even hailed as heroes. And today the field is covered with many acres of rice.

"Rivers are a lifeline for this region, and our ancestors knew that," Kibria says as he walks an embankment. "Opening the fields connects everything. It raises the land level to make up for the rise in sea level. It preserves livelihoods and diversifies the kinds of crops that we can grow. It also keeps thousands of farmers and fishermen from giving up and moving to Dhaka."

But every adaptation, no matter how clever, is only temporary. Even at its sharply reduced rate of growth, Bangladesh's population will continue to expand—to perhaps more than 250 million by the turn of the next century—and some of its land will continue to dissolve. Where will all those people live, and what will they do for a living?

Many millions of Bangladeshis are already working abroad, whether in Western countries, in places such as Saudi Arabia and the United Arab Emirates, or in India, where millions fled during Bangladesh's 1971 war of independence against Pakistan and never returned. Millions more have slipped across the frontier in the decades since, prompting social unrest and conflict. Today India seems determined to close and fortify its border, girding against some future mass migration of the type hypothesized in Washington. It's building a 2,500-mile security fence along the border, and security guards have routinely shot people crossing illegally into India. Interviews with families of victims suggest that at least some of the dead were desperate teenagers seeking

You should take a picture of this place and show it to people driving big cars in your country. **Tell them it's a preview** of what South Florida will look like in 40 years.

to help their families financially. They had been shot smuggling cattle from India, where the animals are protected by Hinduism, to Muslim Bangladesh, where they can fetch up to $40 a head.

But if ten million climate refugees were ever to storm across the border into India, Maj. Gen. Muniruzzaman says, "those trigger-happy Indian border guards would soon run out of bullets." He argues that developed countries—not just India—should be liberalizing immigration policies to head off such a chilling prospect. All around Bangladesh bright, ambitious, well-educated young people are plotting their exit strategies.

And that's not such a bad idea, says Mohammed Mabud, a professor of public health at Dhaka's North South University and president of the Organization for Population and Poverty Alleviation. Mabud believes that investing in educating Bangladeshis would not only help train professionals to work within the country but also make them desirable as immigrants to other countries—sort of a planned brain drain. Emigration could relieve some of the pressure that's sure to slam down in the decades ahead. It's also a way to bolster the country's economy; remittances sent back by emigrants account for 11 percent of the country's GDP. "If people can go abroad for employment, trade, or education and stay there for several years, many of them will stay," he says. By the time climate change hits hardest, the population of Bangladesh could be reduced by 8 to 20 million people—if the government makes out-migration a more urgent priority.

For now, the government seems more interested in making climate adaptation a key part of its national development strategy. That translates, roughly, into using the country's environmental woes as leverage in

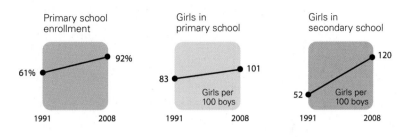

Girl Power
National efforts have raised primary school enrollment to 16.7 million students, with an emphasis on girls, who now outnumber boys in school.

NGM ART
SOURCE: GOVERNMENT OF BANGLADESH

Primary school enrollment

61% 92%

1991 2008

Girls in primary school

83 101

Girls per 100 boys

1991 2008

Girls in secondary school

52 120

Girls per 100 boys

1991 2008

persuading the industrialized world to offer increased levels of aid. It's a strategy that's helped sustain Bangladesh throughout its short, traumatic history. Since independence, it has received tens of billions of dollars in international aid commitments. And as part of the accord produced at the United Nations Climate Change Conference in Copenhagen in 2009, nations of the developed world committed to a goal of $100 billion a year by 2020 to address the needs of poor countries on the front lines of climate change. Many in Bangladesh believe its share should be proportionate to its position as one of the countries most threatened.

"Climate change has become a kind of business, with lots of money flying around, lots of consultants," says Abu Mostafa Kamal Uddin, former program manager for the government's Climate Change Cell. "During the global financial meltdown, trillions of dollars were mobilized to save the world's banks," he says. "What's wrong with helping the poor people of Bangladesh adapt to a situation we had nothing to do with creating?"

Two years after the cyclone, Munshiganj is still drying out. Nasir Uddin and his neighbors are struggling to wring the salt water out of their psyches, rebuild their lives, and avoid being eaten by the tigers that prowl the village at night, driven from the adjacent Sundarbans mangrove forest in search of easy prey. Attacks have risen as population and environmental

pressures have increased. Dozens of residents around Munshiganj have perished or been wounded in recent years—two died the week I was there—and some of the attacks occurred in broad daylight.

"It's bad here, but where else can we go?" Uddin says, surveying the four-foot-high mud platform where he's planning to rebuild his house with an interest-free loan from an NGO. This time he's using wood, which floats, instead of mud. The rice fields around his house are full of water, much of it brackish, and most local farmers have begun raising shrimps or crabs in the brine. Deep wells in the village have gone salty too, he says, forcing people to collect rainwater and apply to NGOs for a water ration, which is delivered by truck to a tank in the village and carried home in aluminum jugs, usually balanced on the heads of young women. "You should take a picture of this place and show it to people driving big cars in your country," says Uddin's neighbor Samir Ranjan Gayen, a short, bearded man who runs a local NGO. "Tell them it's a preview of what South Florida will look like in 40 years."

As the people of Munshiganj can attest, there's no arguing with the sea, which is coming for this land sooner or later. And yet it's hard to imagine millions of Bangladeshis packing up and fleeing en masse to India, no matter how bad things become. They'll likely adapt until the bitter end, and then, when things become impossible, adapt a little more. It's a matter of national mentality—a fierce

RESILIENT SPIRITS

Children play on in Jaliakhali, a village devastated by Cyclone Aila in 2009. That storm sent residents racing for one of thousands of recently built cyclone shelters, many of which double as community centers.

instinct for survival combined with a willingness to put up with conditions the rest of us might not.

Abdullah Abu Sayeed, a literacy advocate, explains it this way: "One day I was driving on one of the busiest streets in Dhaka—thousands of vehicles, all of them in a hurry—and I almost ran over a little boy, no more than five or six years old, who was fast asleep on the road divider in the middle of traffic. Cars were whizzing by, passing just inches from his head. But he was at peace, taking a nap in some of the craziest traffic in the world. That's Bangladesh. We are used to precarious circumstances, and our expectations are very, very low. It's why we can adapt to just about anything."

Discussion Questions

- What is a climate refugee? What types of climate change-driven events can lead to a group of people becoming refugees?

- What are some effects of the relocation of large numbers of people due to climate change?

- What portion of the world's population lives in close proximity to the coast?

- In Bangladesh, what changes have been associated with climate change?

Challenges and Solutions

Identify one or more consequences of climate change for Bangladesh. Propose two to three possible solutions to this issue and build an argument for the best, most realistic and socially acceptable solution.

Social Implications

Identify the social implications of climate change for Bangladeshis and how various stakeholders or interest groups might be affected (e.g. char dwellers, city dwellers, India, etc.). Choose one of these groups and explore their perspective. Assume that this group is taking their issue to the annual global climate change summit, and they wish to issue a press release about their issues and concerns. Write that press release and either a) submit it as a paper, b) give a group presentation to the course, or c) post it to the course blog as directed by your instructor.

CAN CHINA GO GREEN?

China now produces more of the emissions that drive climate change than any other nation, yet at the same time, the country is embracing renewable energy. Despite these efforts, the unprecedented growth of the economy has led to dramatic increases in pollution.

As you read "Can China Go Green?" consider the following questions:

- As economic development proceeds, what is happening to per capita carbon emissions among the Chinese people?
- How does economic growth compare to China's commitment to reducing carbon emissions as a national priority?
- When do experts predict that China's emissions will peak?
- What is the role of environmental groups in Chinese society?
- Why does the development of China play such a pivotal role in the future of global climate change?

A coal yard in northern China comes with a Buddha. Coal reserves could run low in a few decades, making green energy in China a must.

CAN CHINA GO GREEN?

By Bill McKibben

Photographs by Greg Girard

China's hurry-up approach to weaning itself from fossil fuels finds a sleek symbol in a bullet train at Shanghai's Hongqiao Railway Station, its 220-mile-an-hour speeds awing travelers. Within a few years the country will have as much high-speed track—some 8,000 miles—as the rest of the world combined.

NO OTHER COUNTRY
IS INVESTING SO HEAVILY
IN CLEAN ENERGY.
BUT NO OTHER COUNTRY BURNS AS MUCH COAL
TO FUEL ITS ECONOMY.

Rizhao, in Shandong Province, is one of the hundreds of Chinese cities gearing up to really grow. The road into town is eight lanes wide, even though at the moment there's not much traffic. But the port, where great loads of iron ore arrive, is bustling, and Beijing has designated the shipping terminal as the "Eastern bridgehead of the new Euro-Asia continental bridge." A big sign exhorts the residents to "build a civilized city and be a civilized citizen."

In other words, Rizhao is the kind of place that has scientists around the world deeply worried—China's rapid expansion and new-found wealth are pushing carbon emissions ever higher. It's the kind of growth that helped China surge past the United States in the past decade to become the world's largest source of global warming gases.

And yet, after lunch at the Guangdian Hotel, the city's chief engineer, Yu Haibo, led me to the roof of the restaurant for another view. First we clambered over the hotel's solar-thermal system, an array of vacuum tubes that takes the sun's energy and turns it into all the hot water the kitchen and 102 rooms

On top of every single building for blocks around a similar solar array sprouted.

can possibly use. Then, from the edge of the roof, we took in a view of the spreading skyline. On top of every single building for blocks around a similar solar array sprouted. Solar is in at least 95 percent of all the buildings, Yu said proudly. "Some people say 99 percent, but I'm shy to say that."

Whatever the percentage, it's impressive—outside Honolulu, no city in the U.S. breaks single digits or even comes close. And Rizhao's solar water heaters are not an aberration. China now leads the planet in the installation of renewable energy technology—its turbines catch the most wind, and its factories produce the most solar cells.

We once thought of China as the "yellow peril" and then the "red menace." Now the colors are black and green. An epic race is on, and if you knew how the race would come out—if you knew whether or how fast China could wean itself off coal and tap the sun and wind—then you'd have the single most important data point of our century. The outcome

Adapted from "Can China Go Green?" by Bill McKibben: National Geographic Magazine, June 2011.

of that race will determine how bad global warming is going to get. And right now the answer is still up in the air.

Literally up in the air. Visitors to China are instantly struck, of course, by the pollution shrouding every major city. Slowly those skies are clearing a little, at least in places like Beijing and Shanghai, as heavy industry is modernized or moved out of town. And the government has shut down many of the smallest and filthiest coal-fired power plants. Indeed, the country now leads the world in building what engineers call supercritical power stations, which produce far less smog than many of the hulking units still online in the U.S. Presumably China will get steadily cleaner as it gets richer—that's been the story elsewhere.

But—and it's a crucial but—you can clean the air without really cleaning the air. The most efficient coal-fired power plants may not pour as much particulate matter, sulfur dioxide, and nitrogen oxides into the atmosphere, but they still produce enormous quantities of carbon dioxide. Invisible, odorless, generally harmless to humans—and the very thing that's warming the planet. The richer China gets, the more it produces, because most of the things that go with wealth come with a gas tank or a plug. Any Chinese city is ringed with appliance stores; where once they offered electric fans, they now carry vibrating massage chairs.

"People are moving into newly renovated apartments, so they want a pretty, new fridge," a clerk told me. "People had a two-door one, and now they want a three-door." The average Shanghainese household already has 1.9 air conditioners, not to mention 1.2 computers. Beijing registers 20,000 new cars a month. As Gong Huiming, a transportation program officer at the nonprofit Energy Foundation in Beijing, put it: "Everyone wants to get the freedom and the faster speed and the comfort of a car."

Change (and CO₂) in the Air
Burning more than three billion tons of coal a year—more than the U.S., Europe, and India combined—China tops the world in emissions of CO_2 and other atmosphere-warming gases. To slow emissions without impeding its supercharged economic growth, the nation has also become a leader in clean energy, generating nearly 20 percent of its electricity from renewable sources, mostly hydro and wind.

Greenhouse gas emissions
Total emissions in gigatons of CO_2, 2007

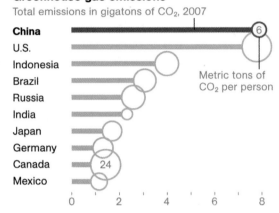

Metric tons of CO_2 per person

Electricity production from renewable sources
Billion kilowatt hours a year, 2008

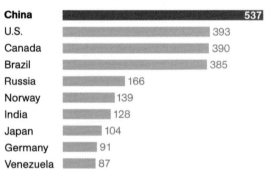

China	537
U.S.	393
Canada	390
Brazil	385
Russia	166
Norway	139
India	128
Japan	104
Germany	91
Venezuela	87

LAWSON PARKER AND KAITLIN M. YARNALL, NGM STAFF

SOURCES: MCKINSEY & COMPANY; POPULATION REFERENCE BUREAU; U.S. ENERGY INFORMATION ADMINISTRATION

That Chinese consumer revolution has barely begun. As of 2007, China had 22 cars for every 1,000 people, compared with 451 in the U.S. Once you leave the major cities, highways are often deserted and side roads are still filled with animals pulling carts. "Mostly, China's concentrated on industrial development so far," said Deborah Seligsohn, who works in Beijing for the Washington, (Continued on page 111)

An instant suburb of high-rises shoots up on the outskirts of the wealthy coal-mining city of Ordos in Inner Mongolia. The feverish growth of urban areas, with their energy-hungry buildings and appliances, has contributed to a tripling of China's power demand since 2000. In Zhenbeipu consumers grab coupons for free cell phones.

What doesn't go up in smoke ends up in a landfill as a truck dumps a load of ash from a coal-fired power plant visible on the horizon in Shizuishan. A 2010 Greenpeace report cites toxic coal ash as China's largest source of solid industrial waste, dispersed by wind and rain into the environment.

Under a bright sky near Shizuishan, a technician makes the rounds of China's first large-scale solar farm. Connected to the grid in 2009, the plant provides ten megawatts of electricity, enough for 10,000 homes. Two-thirds of China's vast land is ideal for solar power.

China's power plants, 2010

Renewable-energy plants are numerous, but most power is still generated by coal.

● One power plant

SOLAR ●● WIND

COAL

NUCLEAR— GAS

OTHER

HYDRO

Dots do not reflect geographic location.

China's power generation, terawatt-hours

	Total
2005	2,503
2030	9,256

Other Hydro Nuclear Gas Coal
Wind
Solar

A Coal-fueled Country

Despite aggressive growth in alternative energy, China will have to burn even more coal to power its booming economy. A forecast for 2030 (above) indicates that if China meets current policy commitments, coal will continue to supply 70 percent of its energy, double the amount used now. To emit no more greenhouse gases in 2030 than today, China would have to rely on green energy for two-thirds of its power generation.

NOTE: ONE TERAWATT-HOUR = 1 BILLION KILOWATT-HOURS. ONE KILOWATT-HOUR WILL POWER A 100-WATT LIGHTBULB FOR TEN HOURS.

LAWSON PARKER AND KAITLIN M. YARNALL, NGM STAFF

SOURCES: PLATTS/UDI WORLD ELECTRIC POWER PLANTS DATABASE; McKINSEY & COMPANY

(Continued from page 104) D.C.-based World Resources Institute. Those steel mills and cement plants have produced great clouds of carbon, and the government is working to make them more efficient. As the country's industrial base matures, their growth will slow. Consumers, on the other hand, show every sign of speeding up, and certainly no Westerner is in a position to scold.

Bill Valentino, a sustainability executive with the pharmaceutical giant Bayer who has long been based in Beijing, recently taught a high school class at one of the international schools. He had his students calculate their average carbon footprint, and they found that if everyone on the planet lived as they did, it would take two to four Earths' worth of raw materials to meet their needs. So they were already living unsustainable lives. Valentino—an expat American who flies often—then did the same exercise and found that if the whole world adopted his lifestyle, we'd require more than five planet Earths.

China has made a low-carbon economy a priority, but no one is under any illusion about the country's chief aim. By most estimates, China's economy needs to grow at least 8 percent a year to ensure social stability and continued communist rule. If growth flags, Chinese may well turn rebellious; there are estimates of as many as 100,000 demonstrations and strikes already each year. Many of them are to protest land takeovers, bad working conditions, and low wages, so the government's main hope is to keep producing enough good jobs to absorb a population still pouring out of the poor provinces with high hopes for urban prosperity.

Increasingly, though, Chinese anger is directed at the environmental degradation that has come with that growth. On one trip I drove through a village north of Beijing where signs strung across the road decried a new gold mine for destroying streams. A few miles later I came to the mine itself, where earlier that day peasants had torn up the parking lot, broken the windows, and scrawled graffiti across the walls. A Chinese government-sponsored report estimates that environmental abuse reduced the country's GDP growth by nearly a quarter in 2008. The official figures may say the economy is growing roughly 10 percent each year, but dealing with the bad air and water and lost farmland that come with that growth pares the figure to 7.5 percent. In 2005 Pan Yue, vice minister of environmental protection, said the country's economic "miracle will end soon, because the environment can no longer keep pace." But his efforts to incorporate a "green GDP" number into official statistics ran into opposition from Beijing.

"Basically," said one Beijing-based official who refused to be identified (itself a reminder of how sensitive these topics are), "China seeks every drop of fuel—every kilowatt and every kilojoule it can get a hold of—for growth." So the question becomes, what will that growth look like?

One thing it already looks like is: big and empty. Ordos, in Inner Mongolia, may be the fastest growing city in China; even by Chinese standards it has an endless number of construction cranes building an endless number of apartment blocks. The city's great central plaza looks as large as Tiananmen Square in Beijing, and towering statues of local-boy-made-good Genghis Khan rise from the concrete plain, dwarfing the few scattered tourists who have made the trek here. There's a huge new theater, a modernist museum, and a remarkable library built to look like leaning books. Coal built this Dubai-on-the-steppe. The area boasts one-sixth of the nation's total reserves, and as a result, the city's per capita income had risen to $20,000 by 2009. (The local government has set a goal of $25,000 by 2012.) It's the kind of place that needs some environmentalists.

And indeed it has at least one. In the neighboring city of Baotou, a steelmaking center whose mines also supply half the planet's rare earth minerals, I found Ding Yaoxian ensconced in the headquarters of the nonprofit Baotou City Environment Federation, on the second floor of a day center for retired party cadres, who were playing badminton on the mezzanine. Director

Ding is one of the most cheerful and engaging Chinese I've ever met; he's needed every bit of charisma to build his association into a real force, numbering by his account a million area citizens. Issued little green identity cards, they serve as a kind of volunteer police force. "If people from the association see someone spilling trash, they go and sit on their doorstep," Ding said. "The government can't have eyes everywhere. A voluntary organization can put more pressure on. It can shame."

But the campaigns the group focuses on most of the time make clear how nascent environmental concern in China still is. They've handed out a million reusable shopping bags—but also hundreds of thousands of small folding paper cups, so that people will stop spitting on the street. One minor victory: When showing those hundreds of thousands of new condo units, real estate agents used to hand customers plastic booties to go over their dirty shoes; now they supply washable cloth socks. The association has tried to introduce the concept of garage sales, in a country where secondhand goods carry a stigma. And members have launched a big effort to teach Inner Mongolians to smile. "In the West people are happy and smiling, and that makes people feel positive," Ding said. His deputy, Feng Jingdong, added, "We tell them, Use your personality to get people to enjoy themselves instead of using resources." The three of us were eating a delicious lunch at a nearby restaurant (lamb is the staple here), and when we were finished, Ding made sure to ask for a doggie bag. "That's one of our campaigns," he said. "Before, it felt like you lost face if you did that."

There was one truly significant sign of greening long under way in the region: a massive tree-planting campaign designed to hold the fragile soil in place. Flatbed trucks packed with seedlings were the second most common

China's green effort is being overwhelmed by the sheer scale of the coal-fueled growth. It's a dark picture.

sight along area roads (outnumbered ten to one, it seemed, by trucks carrying coal from the mines). Ding estimated that he'd planted 100,000 trees with his own hands. "It used to be very dusty here, with lots of sandstorms," he said. "But we had 312 blue sky days last year, and every year there are more."

In search of further reassurance that China's booming growth held real seeds of environmental possibility, I drove 170 miles south of Beijing to the (redundancy alert) booming city of Dezhou. Approaching along National Highway 104, I got a sudden glimpse of one of the world's most remarkable buildings, the Sun-Moon Mansion. It looks like a convention center surrounded by the rings of Saturn, great tracks of solar panels providing all its hot water and electricity. Behind the hotel, a sister building serves as the headquarters of Himin Solar Corporation, which claims to have installed more renewable energy than any other company on Earth. (Chinese enterprises are sometimes the beneficiaries of largesse from Beijing, such as low-interest loans that may never need to be repaid in full.)

Himin's main products are those humble solar-thermal tubes that covered the rooftops in Rizhao. And as it turns out, they cover a lot of other real estate. Huang Ming, who founded the company, estimates that it's erected more than 160 million square feet of solar water heaters. "That means 60 million families, maybe 250 million people altogether—almost the population of the United States," he said. Huang, an ebullient fellow in faded black Dockers who used to be a petroleum engineer, sells some of the best solar-thermal systems in China, but even he admits that it's fairly simple technology. He says that the key to his company's success has been opening people's minds, which it's done with revival-style marketing campaigns that *(Continued on page 119)*

(Continued on page 119)

A perfect site for wind and solar farms, the smoky factories around Shizuishan rely on coal-fired power plants (top), a legacy of Mao Zedong's directive in the 1950s to move industry inland against the threat of foreign attack. Day laborers (bottom) easily find work sorting coal from area mines.

Inside Beijing's first American-style mall, one of the largest anywhere, more than 500 shops vie for customers. Unleashed demand for must-have items like cars and air conditioners is turning China into the world's biggest energy consumer.

Scenery for the industrial age, the cooling towers at the Xinglongzhuang power station mark one of China's first efforts to generate electricity from recycled coal-mining waste. Building an average of one coal-fired plant a week, China is outfitting many with the latest pollution-cutting technology.

The roads of China bear witness to the struggles of energies past and future. In Shaanxi Province coal trucks jam traffic for hours on their way to power plants near eastern cities. In Beijing a tractor trailer with two giant turbine blades is allowed to travel only at night as it rolls toward a wind farm 300 miles away in Inner Mongolia.

(Continued from page 112) storm one city at a time. "We do road showing, lecturing, PowerPointing," he said. And now they're harnessing the power of sightseeing too: The Sun-Moon Mansion is merely the anchor of a vast solar city that will soon include a solar "4-D" cinema, a solar video-game hall, a huge solar-powered Ferris wheel, and solar-powered boats to rent from a solar marina.

The company showroom, Feel It Hall, captures a few contradictions. The solar panels heat water for hot tubs and have giant flat-screen TVs above each. But that's the only way to sell the idea of renewable energy, Huang insisted, as he described the gigantic apartment towers he's building on the edge of town, with racks of solar panels that curve like the back of a dragon. "At night that's what you see—a floating dragon," he said. "So many developers come to our Solar Valley to copy from us, to learn from us. That's just what I wanted."

He's especially happy that some of those visitors come from abroad. Dezhou hosted the International Solar Cities World Congress in 2010, and he's set up an international-experts mansion for visiting dignitaries. "If all the people of the U.S.A. enjoyed solar hot water, Obama would win five Nobel Prizes!" he said. But it's going to take a while for America to catch up. Most of the U.S.'s minuscule capacity is used to heat swimming pools. Jimmy Carter had solar water heaters installed on the roof of the White House in 1979, but they came down in the Ronald Reagan years; new ones are due to go up this year.

It's not the only instance of the Chinese taking an American lead and running with it. Suntech has emerged as one of the top two leading makers of solar photovoltaic panels in the world. New employees are added weekly, and on their first day on the job they watch Al Gore in *An Inconvenient Truth*. The young tour guide showing me around the company's headquarters in Wuxi, near Shanghai, paused

China's growth opens real opportunities for environmental progress—not just solar panels and wind turbines.

by the photos of solar panels at base camp on Mount Everest and the portrait of her boss, Shi Zhengrong, named by *Time* as one of its "heroes of the environment." "It's not only a job," she said, a tear welling in her eye. "I have…mission!"

Of course, that tear might have come in part from the air. Wuxi was among the dirtiest cities I'd ever visited: The 100-degree-Fahrenheit air was almost impossible to breathe. The solar array that forms the front of the Suntech headquarters slanted up to catch the sun's rays. Because of the foul air, it operated at only about 50 percent of its potential output.

In the end, anecdote can take you only so far. Even data are often suspect in China, where local officials have a strong incentive to send rosy pictures off to Beijing. But here's what we know: China is growing at a rate no big country has ever grown at before, and that growth is opening real opportunities for environmental progress. Because it's putting up so many new buildings and power plants, the country can incorporate the latest technology more easily than countries with more mature economies. It's not just solar panels and wind turbines. For instance, some 25 cities are now putting in or expanding subway lines, and high-speed rail tracks are spreading in every direction. All that growth takes lots of steel and cement and hence pours carbon into the air—but in time it should drive down emissions.

That green effort, though, is being overwhelmed by the sheer scale of the coal-fueled growth. So for the time being, China's carbon emissions will continue to soar. I talked with dozens of energy experts, and not one of them predicted emissions would peak before 2030. Is there anything that could move that 2030 date significantly forward? I asked one expert in charge of a clean-energy program. "Everyone's looking, and no one is seeing anything," he said.

Even reaching a 2030 peak may depend in part on the rapid adoption of technology for taking carbon dioxide out of the exhaust from coal-fired power plants and parking it underground in played-out mines and wells. No one knows yet if this can be done on the scale required. When I asked one scientist charged with developing such technology to guess, he said that by 2030 China might be sequestering 2 percent of the carbon dioxide its power plants produce.

Which means, given what scientists now predict about the timing of climate change, the greening of China will probably come too late to prevent more dramatic warming, and with it the melting of Himalayan glaciers, the rise of the seas, and the other horrors Chinese climatologists have long feared.

It's a dark picture. Altering it in any real way will require change beyond China—most important, some kind of international agreement that transforms the economics of carbon. At the moment China is taking green strides that make sense for its economy. "Why would they want to waste energy?" Deborah Seligsohn of the World Resources Institute asked, adding that "if the U.S. changed the game in a fundamental way—if it really committed to dramatic reductions—then China would look beyond its domestic interests and perhaps go much further." Perhaps it would embrace more expensive and speedier change. In the meantime China's growth will blast onward, a roaring fire that throws off green sparks but burns with ominous heat.

"To change people's minds is a very big task," Huang Ming said as we sat in the Sun-Moon Mansion. "We need time, we need to be patient. But the situation will not give us time." A floor below, he's built a museum for busts and paintings of his favorite world figures: Voltaire, Brutus, Molière, Michelangelo, Gandhi, Pericles, Sartre. If he—or anyone else—can somehow help green beat black in this epic Chinese race, he'll deserve a hallowed place near the front of that pantheon.

Discussion Questions

- Which nation produces the most emissions that drive climate change? How has this changed in recent years?

- What is the relationship between the growing prosperity of the Chinese and carbon emissions?

- Refer to the graph on page 104 and compare the total carbon dioxide emissions of the top-polluting nations with their per capita emissions.

- With such significant efforts to incorporate alternative energy sources, such as solar, why are China's carbon emissions continuing to grow?

- Evaluate the assertion that developing economies have a greater ability to adopt renewable energy technologies than developed countries.

Challenges and Solutions

Identify one or more specific reasons for China's continued increase in greenhouse gas emissions. Propose two to three possible interventions that could lead to a reduction in emissions and build an argument for the best, most realistic and socially acceptable solution.

Social Implications

Identify the social implications of China's continued increase in greenhouse gas emissions and discuss how various stakeholders mentioned in the article might be affected (e.g. the government, which needs to maintain economic growth; local environmental groups; etc.). Choose one of these groups and explore their perspective. Assume that this group is taking their issue to the annual global climate change summit, and they wish to issue a press release about their issues and concerns. Write that press release and either a) submit it as a paper, b) give a group presentation to the course, or c) post it to the course blog as directed by your instructor.